D1407939

Corporate
Public Relations

A NEW HISTORICAL PERSPECTIVE

based on whether or a corporation – has can you understand a public understand a situation when obliquely is the occur – talkin Rees or talkin true – one min same?

COMMUNICATIONS

A series of volumes edited by
Dolf Zillmann and Jennings Bryant

Corporate
Public Relations

A NEW HISTORICAL PERSPECTIVE

Marvin N. Olasky

THE UNIVERSITY OF TEXAS AT AUSTIN

LEA LAWRENCE ERLBAUM ASSOCIATES, PUBLISHERS
Hillsdale, New Jersey   Hove and London

Lawrence Erlbaum Associates, Inc., Publishers
365 Broadway
Hillsdale, New Jersey 07642

Library of Congress Cataloging-in-Publication Data

Olasky, Marvin N.
    Corporate public relations

    (Communication)
    Bibliography: p.
    Includes indexes.
    1. Public relations—United States—History.
    I. Title.   II. Series: Communication (Hillsdale, N.J.)
HD59.6.U604   1987   659.2'0973   87-3551
ISBN 0-8058-0052-2

Printed in the United States of America
10 9 8 7 6 5 4 3 2

For Susan

CONTENTS

PREFACE

This book is written for four sets of people who want to think for themselves.

First, it is for public relations practitioners, professors and students who want to understand why corporate public relations is sinking deeper into ethical and political quicksand. The historical perspective contained in this book is a branch held out for grasping and eventual safety.

Second, it is for procompetition corporate executives and managers who look at their companies' public relations departments and say with exasperation, "What's going on?" This history will help them to understand why some public relations managers work against private enterprise objectives.

Third, it is for historians of media and society who want to know more about the development of a crucial part of American culture, and do not want to settle for histories either decrying big business as evil or hailing it as man's savior.

Fourth, it is for political conservatives and libertarians. This is a probusiness book. For that reason, it must criticize those corporate public relations activities designed to minimize competition through creation of a government–business partnership, supposedly in the public interest. Probusiness citizens in the 1990s may have to oppose plans of some large corporate bureaucracies.

This book was created through the support of four groups of people who encouraged *me* to think for myself.

First, family. *Corporate Public Relations* is dedicated to my wife Susan: She provided not only love but wise counsel. My children Peter, David, and Daniel helped me to remember that there is more to life than writing books, and my parents Eli and Ida Olasky early on taught me to love reading books.

Second, colleagues. Chairman Max McCombs and other professors in the Department of Journalism of The University of Texas at Austin helped to establish a congenial writing and teaching environment. Dwight Teeter in particular has been a good friend. Former colleagues and supervisors in the Du Pont Company taught me much about organization and management.

Third, manuscript readers and editors. Jim Grunig, Joe McKerns, Bill Stott, Paul Weaver, and several anonymous reviewers read parts of the manuscript at various stages. They made useful comments and helped me to avoid numerous blunders. Earlier versions of chapters were published in *Public Relations Review*, *Public Relations Quarterly*, the *Wall Street Journal*, *Journalism History*, *Journalism Monographs*, *Business and Society Review*, *Journal of Mass Media Ethics*, *Reason*, and the *Journal of Popular Film and Television*. Five of the chapters were presented as papers at annual meetings of the Association for Education in Journalism and Mass Communication. I appreciate the understanding of journal editors and AEJMC research committee members.

Fourth, supporters within public relations and business. Every occupational group has its sensitivities, but public relations is notorious for its squads of cheerleaders who yell "Knock him down, hit him again, harder, harder," whenever anyone dares to criticize. For that reason, I especially appreciate the interest of Howard Penn Hudson and Paul Swift of *Public Relations Quarterly*, George Pearson of Koch Industries, the loyal opposition at Du Pont, and others in communications and corporate management who bravely refuse to bend the knee to some contemporary idols.

Most of all, I appreciate God's Providence.

Marvin N. Olasky

INTRODUCTION

Asking Basic Questions

A decade ago, in an article entitled "The Limits of Progressive Journalism History," Joseph McKerns noted that, "The dominant interpretative approach, or paradigm, to the history of journalism has been the Progressive interpretation . . . " McKerns contended that the Progressive view of linear improvement in American journalism over the years, with a goal of onwards and upwards to liberalism, has been superficial at best.[1] McKerns was accurate in his reporting and in his critique. With others sharing his perspective, useful reinterpretations of journalism history began to emerge.

No such renaissance, though, has occurred in that subset of journalism history known as public relations history. The Progressive interpretation continues to dominate general concepts of public relations development in two ways.

First, all of us who practice or teach in the field are familiar with the common view that American public relations practice has improved sharply since the "press agent" era of the late 19th or early 20th century.

Second, we have all listened to numerous sermonettes about how corporations have better served "the public interest" by spending more time relating to their public (or "publics"), practicing "boundary spanning," developing professional contributions functions, and learning to dicker and deal in Washington.

One problem faced by apologists for bigger and better public relations is that the reputation of public relations seems to be getting worse rather than better. In recent years, public relations practitioners have been regularly labeled "high-paid errand boys and buffers for management," "tools of the top brass," "hucksters," "parrots," "impotent, evasive, egomaniacal and lying."[2]

A deeper problem is that many of the uncomplimentary references are based on ample evidence. When critics say that "telling half the truth is an integral part" of public relations,[3] examples are not hard to find: Practitioners use terms such as "revenue excess" for "profit," "price enhancement" for "price increase," "period of accelerated negative growth" for "increased losses," and "involuntary conversion of a 727" for the crash of a Boeing airplane.[4]

A common fault today is that public relations workers who want to be honest and productive (and that, in my experience, includes the majority) often have no background in the actual history of their occupation. A little exposure to the standard onwards-and-upwards history of public relations can be a dangerous thing because it leads to excuses such as "Give us time," or "We're a young profession." Public relations, however, is actually a venerable occupation (the second oldest in the eyes of some critics). If little improvement has emerged over the years, the reasons for stagnation should be investigated.

A different interpretation of public relations history, particularly in its corporate practice, might help us to understand why current problems and perspectives have arisen. This book, through its analysis of landmark cases in public relations (including the use of public relations in the railroad, telephone, movie, and steel industries) and its critique of the philosophies of innovators such as Ivy Lee and Edward Bernays, provides that different analysis. It does not pretend to be an overall history of public relations and corporate social/cultural concerns, but it does tell a story of convoluted philosophy and tawdry practice.

That story is this: For over a century, many major corporate public relations leaders have worked diligently to kill free enterprise by promoting government-big business collaboration. Over and over again, many corporate public relations executives have supported economic regulation with the goal of eliminating smaller competitors and insuring their own profits. They have sold such restrictions on freedom by promising better service, but their frequent inability to deliver has left a residue of public disbelief in the promises of corporate America.

My rethinking of American corporate public relations began during five years of public relations work at Du Pont and continued through studies of the United States Constitution. I realized that we live in a nation founded on the importance of private interests and private relations; "good fences make good neighbors" was Robert Frost's poetic translation of the debate over the Constitution. Two hundred years later, it seemed time to ask once again some basic questions about the relationship of public relations to private enterprise.

I began by learning how James Madison and his colleagues grew up with British speeches about the importance of the "public interest." They saw that landowners who worked hard at improving property but did not mind their public relations could lose everything "for the public good." Astute citizens were careful to throw parties for and bribes at magistrates with power to damage their interests.[5]

Madison and his colleagues saw that authorities allowed only those economic activities that were seen to benefit the public interest. Constitutional authors were so sick of such restrictions that they decided to strictly limit the federal government's role. They would not support creation of a national university or other institutions for furthering literature or art, even though there were clear "public interest" benefits. They would not give the federal government power to build canals or to regulate stages, clearly in the "public interest."

Most of the Constitution framers' counterparts in the individual states were equally hesitant about suggesting that private parties should do anything else than a sound job at their private tasks. Exceptions occurred, but emphasis during the Republic's early years was always on *private* relations. Madison provided the theoretical base for this consistent political caution: He opposed those who said the United States must give public goals primacy over individual aspirations. Citizens do not have the same passions or interests, he wrote, and any attempt to establish harmony by proclaiming commonalities when none exist is hostile to liberty.[6]

Madison brilliantly proposed an alternative philosophy of social organization: Encourage private interests. Madison argued that the United States must have a wide and competing variety of economic and political interests, all suspicious of each other, all unwilling to enter into agreements to stifle those left out. Madison suggested that public progress was most likely to occur when private interests were pursued. In society as in government, liberty was most likely when competing forces kept each other from becoming too powerful, and therefore allowed individuals to pursue their own private interests without impediment.[7]

The opposition of Madisonian thinking to concepts of "public interest" dominated American politics during the Constitution's first century. Farmers and small businessmen welcomed the protection afforded them by the belief that "little people" and "little places" were just as important as governmental projects. The rule of law rather than public pressure allowed the building of strong fences around private properties.

Strong fences made a strong nation. Early nineteenth-century public relations practitioners such as Amos Kendall based their work on principles of private interest. Their human nature was not any different from the nature of today's practitioners, but they had a different political and theological philosophy. Kendall and others did not try to manipulate others into thinking that what they wanted was in the "public interest." Instead, they tried to restrict government as much as possible to a limited judicial function. Government would involve itself in economic disputes only when one pursuer of private interest was attempting to overwhelm another illegally.

Business blather about public spiritedness was not omnipresent during the early nineteenth century. Instead, business leaders worked under the simple but effective slogans of private relations: "Build better mousetraps" and "Mind your own business." Businessmen had few public relations concerns because they purposefully did not go public very often. Chapter one discusses the public relations history of that ante-bellum era.

All was not sugar and spice, of course. In the transportation industry, a few businessmen for many years tried to pick up government aid whenever they could. Some well-connected individuals in other industries also gained advantage through the public-private partnerships of the day. In several cases the federal government justified particular grants on grounds of military necessity. Nevertheless, the essential concept—private enterprise, private relations—remained intact until 1850.

During the second half of the 19th century, though, several railroad industry executives abandoned the private relations consensus and began using public relations to obtain government support and protection of their enterprises. As we will see in chapters two and three, every railroad public relations problem had a "realistic" solution. Every step was a "logical" one. The short-term result was establishment of a governmental commission to protect the "public interest." The long-term result, because of federal involvement and other factors, was railroad industry debacle.

Early in the 20th century, railroad public relations pathfinders were followed by executives such as Theodore Vail and Samuel Insull, leaders in the telephone and electric utility industries who became adept at using public interest language. They did so to win acceptance for the concept of regulated monopoly.

As chapter four will show, Vail and Insull both encouraged increased regulation "in the public interest," in order to gain and maintain government-backed protection from competitors. Electric utilities and Bell system companies developed enormous public relations staffs to push the regulated monopoly concept. Those practitioners bribed, softsoaped, and schemed, but always defended their actions with a public interest rationale. They proclaimed good will toward mankind while using government to create peace on earth based on stifling the competition.

Ivy Lee, the father of modern public relations according to introductory textbooks, also did his best to reduce competition, in the "public interest." Chapter five shows how he was one of the first public relations practitioners to oppose competitive enterprise through conscious espousal of corporate collaborationism (alliances of large corporations with each other and with the federal government). He combined sophisticated economics with situational ethics developed through assimilation of popularized Darwinian and Freudian thought. Lee was so slick that one could no longer lump public relations workers with the old-time snake oil peddlers. This was public relations progress.

Two public relations campaigns of the 1920s and 1930s demonstrated both the usefulness and the ultimate failure of some of Ivy Lee's techniques. Chapter six shows how the motion-picture industry put off for a decade major public protest, but had to make far-reaching changes when the boiler finally exploded. Chapter seven documents corporate public relations backing for the National Recovery Administration (NRA) campaign of 1933, with the goal of mandating prices that would provide leading corporations with profits without the hardship of competition. The huge NRA public relations push eventually failed as journalists, legislators, and the public saw that job-creating promises were not being kept.

After the movie industry and NRA flops, something better was needed. Chapters eight and nine tell of the public relations strategist, Edward Bernays, who put all the pieces together. Bernays developed and won acceptance for the idea of an American society headed toward chaos unless public relations counselors worked behind the scenes to "manipulate public opinion" (his words, used positively) into harmonious patterns. Truly competitive enterprise was done for, Bernays believed; we must substitute new "sacred dances" for old competitive striving and make sure that government plays the tune.

From the mid-1930s onward, the modern concept of public relations "in the public interest" swept through American industry. Chapter ten describes how public relations added sugar to its drink mix. Chapter eleven examines in greater depth an industry that spent thirty years proclaiming the importance of harmony and public-private partnership, and then found itself undone by public relations success during a 1962 crisis.

Chapter twelve brings the history from the 1960s through the 1980s by showing how corporate public relations increasingly has functioned as part of what we now call strategic planning. Public relations-minded executives often have had as their goal not a fending off of government but a knocking off of competitors by making the public believe that centralization is inevitable and government is a needed protector. All of this was said to be in the public interest, of course, but such activity undercut the basic ethos of competitive enterprise.

The impact on public relations practice of this movement in political philosophy has been severe. Many staffers have been forced to talk out of both sides of their mouths, praising competitive enterprise in boilerplate speeches but developing plans to promote acceptance of cartels.

Great confusion over what is private and what is public has led to great confusion over what information should be made public. Many public relations practitioners have been caught between an ideology-based belief that the public has a right to know all kinds of details in the public interest, and a practical realization that information about a company's internal operations, in a private enterprise economy, must be the company's business.

In practice, this ideological confusion has led to endless attempts to talk around a subject. Questions about internal functioning, instead of receiving a smiling refusal to comment, have been continually sidestepped. Public relations practitioners who have proclaimed the importance of answering reporters' questions cannot readily give a direct "no comment," because they have agreed that those words are illegitimate; therefore, manipulation of reporters to avoid straightforward refusals has become standard procedure.

Chapter thirteen delves deeper into some of the basic public relations questions by showing how public relations encouragement of "social responsibility" concepts has opened up demand for further access into private areas. Falling into a bottomless pit, public relations men and women have been forced to pretend that they stand on liberal ground. For instance, during the recurrent debates over tax preferences, pity the poor speechwriter brought in to explain why tax breaks for esoteric investments are in the public interest. Plausible phrases and apple-polishing apologia come to mind, but at the cost of two-facedness once again.

Two-facedness is hard on individuals as well as institutions. Picture the practitioner working in public relations for a major steel company who is charged with producing statements about the company's continuing commitment to steel. He knows that the company is closing its plants and moving out of the steel business. He knows that the company is lobbying for tax breaks and quotas. But he cannot write that, so he writes subtle lies and further reduces the reputation of public relations, along with his own ability to look in the mirror.

One point worth emphasizing is that many of the frequently-used public relations methods—work the press here, lobby there, contribute here, give a speech about the "public interest" there—have been thoroughly realistic and thoroughly logical in the short-term. But throughout the past century, they have been proven wrong in the long-term for the country as a whole and for individual companies, in many instances. What are the alternatives? That is the subject matter of chapter fourteen and the conclusion. Before we examine possible futures, it is time to begin this reexamination of public relations history by returning to the early 19th century.

CHAPTER ONE

Voluntarism and Restraint: Early 19th-Century Public Relations

Few scholars have attempted to chart the 19th-century ancestors of 20th-century public relations. One of the best monographs, by Alan Raucher in 1958, noted three major antecedents: press agentry, advertising, and the early attempts of business reformers to place private corporations under some degree of public control.[1]

Yet, to understand problems affecting the 20th-century occupation, we need to examine a fourth and neglected aspect of 19th-century public relations: the surge of nonprofessional, spontaneous public relations activity in the United States during the early 19th century.

One example of the difference between decentralized, voluntaristic 19th-century public relations, and the current professionalized model, was the handling of Lafayette's visit to America in 1824 through 1825.

Lafayette, hero of the American Revolution a half century earlier, had both political disappointments and financial difficulties in France. His hope of American-style constitutional government in France was dashed with the reinstatement of the Bourbon monarchy following Napoleon's final downfall. Financially, Lafayette had contributed much from his own pocket for the American Revolution and had then seen his ancestral estates confiscated by the French revolutionary government. In the 1820s Lafayette was excluded from the Chamber of Deputies in France because of his opposition to Bourbon policies.[2]

Meanwhile, during the 1820s the United States was trying to remind itself of its revolutionary principles and was also trying to show the monarchies of Europe that this republican country had grown and come into its own. One of the frequent charges levelled by aristocrats against democracies was that "the mob" had no sense of history, no sense of gratitude to those who had served it, and no sense of the meaning of "virtue," which implied self-sacrifice for the sake of honor.

With Lafayette in trouble and America needing an opportunity to do what was right—to show that a republic could have gratitude and could pass on its heritage to new generations—a unique public relations opportunity presented itself: Lafayette was invited to tour America half a century after the revolutionary triumphs and to see what men and God had wrought.

There was no central planning committee to make the arrangements. Each community invited Lafayette on its own and made preparations to receive him properly as he passed by on the grand tour scheduled by a personal secretary who traveled with the aged Lafayette and by the grand old man's son, George Washington Lafayette. For instance, here is a report of public relations planning in Murfreesborough, North Carolina, as printed in the *Norfolk and Portsmouth Herald* of March 4, 1825:

> On Friday the 25th about noon, we received information that Gen. Lafayette would probably pass through this place, on his way to Raleigh; and being anxious to show him every mark of respect and esteem in their power, the citizens assembled to make such arrangements for his reception and accommodation as the shortness of the notice would allow . . .[3]

The citizens formed three committees: one to meet Lafayette in Summerton, Virginia, and invite him to stop at Murfreesborough; one to arrange for his reception and provide housing; the third to choose a speaker who would make a formal address of welcome. Everything proceeded well. Lafayette was "escorted into town, where he was received under an ARCH, (erected for that purpose, which was handsomely illuminated, and decorated with evergreens)." A Mr. Thomas Maney made the welcoming speech, "Those of us who have risen up in another generation, behold in you the original of that picture of excellence which our fathers have impressed upon our hearts."[4]

The townspeople of Fayetteville, North Carolina also met and voted to establish an invitation committee, an arrangements committee, and a banquet committee. Their invitation noted that Fayetteville had been the first town in America to be named after the revolutionary hero, and Lafayette said that of course he would come. At the banquet, a Judge Toomer gave Lafayette the public relations message, on behalf of the town committee: "We are plain republicans, and cannot greet you with the pomp common on such occasions. Instead of pageantry, we offer you cordiality," and in this way show that "ingratitude is no longer the reproach of republics."[5]

Similarly, the main speaker in Charleston, South Carolina contrasted professional public relations work in ancient Rome with his town's volunteer efforts:

> The triumphal entries of Pompey and of Caesar were but the adulations of a conquered city; followed by victims, gladiators, and spoils. But the voluntary burst of gratitude and admiration, which . . . a whole continent of freedom expresses for the friend of Washington and the rights of man, is without a parallel in the history of mankind.[6]

The fundraising aspects of public relations were also handled in unpaid but competent style. In Savannah, Georgia, members of a volunteer committee produced 500 copies of a brochure, which they sent out to solicit funds for a memorial to Revolutionary War generals Greene and Pulaski. The brochure summarized the "character and services" of the war heroes, then concluded:

> We therefore invite our Fellow-Citizens throughout the state to cooperate with us in this work of duty, that the State of Georgia may give another example to the world that Republics are not unmindful of the obligations which they owe, both to the living and the dead.

The contributions came in on the basis of this frank appeal to a republic's public relations: often the goal was to give an "example to the world."

Not everything went smoothly. At Charleston, South Carolina, the limitations of even careful public relations planning became evident:

> To Dr. James Davis and Professor Henry Nott had been assigned the duty of going about twenty paces in front of the procession to see the path clear and all in fitting order for the tread of the august personage [Lafayette] to follow. Some mischievous boy, at a cross street, threw in an old gander . . . To try to catch the goose was out of the question, as it, of course, would create confusion and unseemly mirth; so he walked, in solitary dignity, poking out his neck from side to side, stopping now and then to give a hiss at the men. The doctor and professor, hats in hand, [were] venturing a mild "shew! shew!" and giving a gentle flourish of their hats to accelerate his movements. The gander would give a "quack! quack!" in return, not improving his pace, but merely resuming the even tenor of his way, and so he led the van to the end of the line.[8]

Still, these were citizen public relations practitioners, and some problems were expected and accepted. In short, throughout the year of Lafayette's American "pilgrimage of liberty," arrangements were made, speeches were written, the press was used artfully, brochures were produced, funds were collected and distributed, public opinion was sounded, and "a good time was had by all," without professional public relations counsel.

Less important events also brought forth the volunteer public relations committee. For instance, one flurry now forgotten by historians occurred in June, 1846, when the unpopular Pope Gregory XVI died at age 81. Americans had been reading how the prisons of the Papal States (consisting at that time of the province of Rome, the Romagne, Umbria, and the Marches) were overflowing with political prisoners, so there was rejoicing when the cardinals' conclave selected Giovanni Mastai Ferretti, a young man with more democratic views, to be the next pope. Ferretti who took the name Pius XI, immediately abolished secret tribunals for political offenders and declared an amnesty for all political prisoners among the eight million persons of the Papal States.

The question for American followers of international news was, how could they tell others that a new era in international politics may have arrived, and how could they best assert their support for the republican forces of Europe? Now, a call would go to Burson–Marsteller, but in 1847 a group of New Yorkers met privately to discuss ways to register public approval of the papal action.

They decided to form a committee of influential men to organize a public meeting: Vanbrugh Livingston became chairman, and Horace Greeley, Theodore Sedgwick, William Cullen Bryant, James W. Gerard and Joseph Avezzana also participated. Several thousand people showed up at the meeting they arranged; New York Mayor William V. Brady spoke of the public support for the Pope's reform efforts. Horace Greeley chaired a volunteer committee to write a letter to the Pope, and that letter was read to the audience:

> We address you not as a Sovereign Pontiff, but as the wise and human Ruler of a once oppressed and discontented, now well-governed and gratefully happy people. We unite in this tribute, not as Catholics, which some of us are while the great number are not, but as . . . lovers of Constitutional Freedom.[9]

The letter was adopted by acclamation, and copies of it were distributed around the United States. That volunteer public relations effort led to resolutions by several legislatures, editorials in newspapers across the country, and a heartening of Europeans fighting for republican and against monarchical principles.

Another typical example of early 19th-century public relations work involved the development of railroads. There were no professional public relations staffers on the nascent railroad lines of the 1830s; nevertheless, public enthusiasm led to the volunteer publication of railroad brochures and booklets.

The first pro-railroad American magazine, for instance, emerged from the hamlet of Rogersville, Tennessee, after a group of excited citizens met to discuss ways to disseminate information on the utility and practicality of railroads. A committee of 20 published "The Railroad Advocate – Conducted by an Association of Gentlemen." The first issue, published on July 4, 1831, advocated "extending the railroad throughout the country" as "an immediate means of encouraging industry and developing the resources of the state."[10]

What could be called railroad "product introductions" were also decentralized, volunteer efforts. For instance, the opening of a railroad from Providence, Rhode Island, to Stonington, Connecticut, on March 10, 1837, was planned by an ad hoc Stonington committee. Committee members arranged for the steamer Narragansett to bring a party of railroad directors and guests from New York to Stonington. They had the guests greeted by the roar of an 18-pound cannon last used against the British in 1814. They put on a banquet at which everyone took turns making toasts, including the following:

> To the ladies of Stonington – may the railroad, the completion of which we are this day called to celebrate, more extensively introduce their claims and virtues to their fellow citizens from Maine to Georgia.[11]

Later on, of course, professionals planned systematic efforts to promote settlement along rail lines moving west. Early railroad enthusiasm, though, was one subset of the voluntarism that amazed French observer Alexis de Tocqueville, author of *Democracy in America* in 1835.

> Americans of all ages, all conditions, and all dispositions constantly form associations. . . . If it is proposed to inculcate some truth or to foster some feeling by the encouragement of a great example, they form a society . . . what political power could ever [do what Americans voluntarily] perform every day with the assistance of the principle of association?[12]

De Tocqueville was impressed not only by voluntarism, but by public relations restraint as well. He noted the existence of strong theological constraints during the 1830s: "While the law permits the Americans to do what they please, religion prevents them from conceiving, and forbids them to commit, what is rash or unjust."[13]

Given our human ability to contemplate wrongdoing, de Tocqueville may have been overoptimistic on the conceiving, but he probably was accurate on the committing. Techniques of opinion manipulation were not unknown in 19th-century America, and some patent medicine advertising of the period reached heights of eloquent but fraudulent persuasion far beyond those yet reached by current television commercializing. Yet when it came to attempting to move men's minds in particular directions concerning the virtues and vices of ideas, or to praise or excoriate particular individuals, there was an unwillingness to serve merely as a "hired gun."

It is vital to understand this if we are to properly appreciate the early 19th-century volunteers, and even some of the individuals frequently cited as predecessors of the modern, professional public relations practitioner. For instance, Amos Kendall of the Jackson administration was criticized by his contemporaries for lower standards than most, but he still knew that honor has value.

One of my favorite Kendall stories concerns his response to a request for public relations assistance from a future United States vice president, Richard M. Johnson: Kendall wrote that, "I shall give Richard my vote, but I shall not be his tool."[14] Historian Claude G. Bowers observed concerning Kendall:

> He promised himself never knowingly to misrepresent; if, through mistake, he did, to rectify the mistake without being asked; never to retract a statement he thought true; to resent an insult in kind; to defend himself, if assaulted, by any means necessary, even to killing, and never to run.[15]

Kendall emphasized a newspaper editor's or publicist's "awful responsibility" to "himself, his Country and his God."[16]

Even P. T. Barnum, often held up as a prototypical manipulator who profited by deceiving the helpless, had a practice far removed from the hidden persuasion that some say has followed. Barnum's hoodwinking in antebellum America was done with a wink, and his practice as well as his consumer guide, *Humbugs of the World,* condemned deceptions which hurt, such as those of lottery sharks and phony auctioneers.[17]

Barnum believed that because a sucker is born every minute, it is up to those who sell either goods or entertainment to exercise restraint and pass up the opportunity to take candy from babies. As Daniel Boorstin has noted in *The Image,* "contrary to popular belief, Barnum's great discovery was not how easy it was to deceive the public, but rather, how much the public enjoyed being deceived. Especially if they could see how it was being done."[18] Barnum was a magician who enjoyed explaining his tricks, not a Great and Powerful Oz who stood behind the curtain with guards to keep away little dogs.

The emphasis on restraint was evident in numerous accounts, including one of the earliest American speeches on record concerning the practice of public relations, that of New Yorker Hugh Smith (1795–1849) before Columbia College alumni in 1842. Smith, discussing the "ethics of persuasion," argued that efforts to influence opinion could be legitimate if they met three criteria: They had to avoid the employment of falsehood, avoid appeals to prejudices and passions, and avoid the "proscription of those who will not fall in with particular opinions or practices."[19]

The decentralist and voluntaristic emphases of early 19th-century public relations have clearly been superseded in this century by paid, concentrated labors. That clock cannot be turned back, but noting that voluntarism was accompanied by restraint is important for two reasons.

First, volunteers would carry out public relations labors because they were believed to be useful, not because they were paid for. They could not be pushed by financial exigency further than they wished to go. Second, even those professionals such as Amos Kendall, who could be hurt financially by refusal to serve as a hired gun, tended to examine opportunities in line with the ethics of the time: They would not be "tools."

Human nature has not changed much over the years, but theological restraint against writing and saying what was not believed may have been stronger then than now. Can the idea of restraint in public relations be brought back? Should it be? Public relations practitioners who are responsible and ethical have a hard time overcoming the popular depiction of the occupation as one made up of those who will do anything for a buck, or at least for big bucks. The past practice of voluntaristic public relations holds before us the concept that individuals should advocate only what they believe.

The lessons of voluntaristic restraint may be limited. It may be easy to say no when the financial future of a practitioner and his or her family is not at stake. Still, without that concept of restrained advocacy, practitioners are prime suspects for the charge against much of contemporary culture leveled by novelist Larry McMurtry:

> One seldom, nowadays, hears anyone described as 'a person of character.' The concept goes with an ideal of maturity, discipline and integration that strongly implies repression: people of character, after all, cannot do just anything, and an ability to do just about anything with just about anyone – in the name, perhaps, of Human Potential – is certainly one of the most *moderne* abilities.[20]

The "ability to do just about anything with just about anyone" is one of the leading contemporary public relations abilities, according to critics of the field. Those critics sometimes exaggerate, but the common attacks may be contrasted with a generalization by Henry Steele Commager concerning the early 19th-century American volunteer: "He had a high sense of honor . . . Words like truth, justice, loyalty, reverence, virtue, and honor meant much to him." Commager may be emphasizing the positive side as some critics of public relations emphasize the negative. But when was the last time we heard someone say about the typical modern, professional practitioner, "He has a high sense of honor"?[21]

CHAPTER TWO

Onto the Gravy Train:
19th-Century Railroad Public Relations

The escape from honor in public relations proceeded first upon railroad tracks. That would have seemed an unlikely prospect in the 1830s, when the U.S. railroad industry started pushing ahead, but in this chapter we will see how standards began to turn around.

Early in the 19th century, according to U.S. presidents at least, one thing was clear: Federal involvement in transportation projects of any kind was to be minimized. James Madison in 1817 vetoed a road-building measure, arguing that federal transportation funding was an unconstitutional foray into state, local, and private relations. Presidents Monroe, Jackson, Tyler, and Polk vetoed similar bills on constitutional grounds.

In several cases, grants for improvements were made by the federal government and justified on grounds of military necessity, but the essential policy remained intact until 1850. This policy of federal noninvolvement was helpful to early railroads. It forced them away from hope of subsidy and into a hard struggle for backers and customers. They responded to competitive need or desire, not planners' ambition or wish.

The Charleston and Hamburg Railroad, for instance, opened in 1833 to connect Charleston, South Carolina, with the Savannah River traffic of Augusta, Georgia. Its purpose was to serve cotton traffic that would otherwise be monopolized by the movement of steamer downriver to the port of Savannah. The Boston and Worcester Railroad opened in 1837 with the similar goal of convincing inland Worcester's trade to head to Boston rather than to Providence.

These works were usually paid for by small businessmen seeking profit.

Henry Williams of the Boston and Worcester Railroad noted about fundraising for his line, "The work was commenced and has been completed by the middling class of the community." Railroad leaders were proud of overcoming obstacles without federal aid. James Boorman, president of the Hudson River Railroad, wrote to his board of directors about a project begun in the 1840s, "In the completion of this work we may justly feel that we have gained a triumph — a great moral triumph."[1]

Beginning about 1850, however, several public relations-minded railroad leaders decided to relinquish the concepts of voluntarism and independence and begin pushing harder for a ride on a federal gravy train. Illinois Central officials in particular demanded a subsidy for building a new road. They wanted more money, not "moral triumphs."

Initially, their attempt received strong opposition. The *American Railroad Journal* complained about the executives' plan for "the *public* to furnish the means necessary to build the road, while *they* pocket the profits." Constitution-minded opponents of the subsidy raised a fundamental question: "Where is the power in this Government to make a donation to A in a manner that presses B into paying double price?"[2]

Illinois Central officials overwhelmed the opposition through an enormous public relations campaign. Lobbyists such as George Billings and Robert Rantoul, Jr., played on the growing concern about an eventual civil war by arguing that a nationally-funded north–south railroad would bind North and South "together so effectually that even the idea of separation" would become unthinkable. They were wrong, of course, but they were not proved wrong until the subsidy was history.[3]

The success of the Illinois Central campaign opened the door to other railroad subsidy-seekers. Between 1852 and the financial crisis of 1857, Congress made grants to 40 railroads. Originally, as with the Lockheed and Chrysler bail-outs of recent years, proponents of subsidy worked hard to justify particular grants. Soon, though, log-rolling became common: The rationale was no longer that a specific project was in the public interest, but that the public interest was generally served by governmental subsidies for railway building.

Opponents to subsidy argued that railroad grants implicitly involved government in income redistribution, but their pleas were overriden. Southern legislators in particular tended to oppose federal grants during the 1850s; when they were absent from Washington during the following decade, railroad lobbyists truly went to work. Grants to the Northern Pacific and dozens of other railroads were enormous. Opponents of railroad public relations were left merely to sputter about "the most monstrous and flagrant attempt to overreach the Government and the people" yet devised.[4]

At this time some railroads became "public–private partnerships" by having government-appointed members of their boards of directors. The Union

Pacific had five federal appointees on its 20-member board shortly after the Civil War. The record of the government directors was not auspicious. One director obtained Union Pacific securities well below market price, violating the terms of his appointment, and another admitted before a Congressional investigating committee that he had winked at deceitful lobbying activities. But the tradition of government involvement in railroad management had begun.

The success of the first railroad campaign led to proposals for expansion and regularization of public relations work. A few railroad executives wanted none of that. George Washington Cass, Jr., president of the Pittsburgh, Fort Wayne and Chicago from 1856 to 1881, opposed plans for what we would now call "media relations" or "governmental relations" staffing.

Cass was pleasurably straightforward in his correspondence. Asked about a journalist, Cass replied, "I agree with you that Gibson knows what he is writing about . . . There is only one way of keeping these fellows quiet if they are disposed to make a noise and that is to buy them up—and this I am not disposed to do." In response to a governmental relations proposal, Cass wrote, "We have no emissary in Washington nor do we care to go into that kind of business. It is quite expensive and very seldom pays."[5]

To almost all public relations suggestions Cass' reply was virtually the same: "Go along minding your business and the Company's and let quarrelsome men look out for themselves." He objected to proposals that railroads gain support from the press by distributing free tickets or "passes" to editors and reporters. Cass, born in 1810, spent many years in the mercantile business in Pennsylvania before becoming involved with railroads during his forties, and he often looked at railroad problems from the perspective of a shipper who wanted to minimize costs and would enjoy having railroads bid for his business.

Cass also was sensitive to railroad overstepping of fundamental political principles for short-term advantage: He wrote that trade monopolies would injure railroad public relations, for "monopolies are always odious under a Republican form of government." When Cass became president for a short time of the Northern Pacific, one member of his board of directors attempted to gain Washington support for a corporate economic endeavor, but Cass insisted that a railroad should be "a responsible body and not a lobby that is pushing the endorsement by the Government of our Bonds."[6]

Cass, however, represented a declining tradition of entrepreneurial independence. Trust-building and "collaborative" enterprise were becoming fashionable in the late 19th century. Correspondence of younger executives who spent virtually their entire careers in the railroad industry shows a deemphasis on competition with each other and a tendency toward collaborative facing of the outside world.

Henry Ledyard was one of the prime advocates of increased railroad public relations. Born in 1844, he started out as a clerk to a Chicago, Burlington & Quincy district superintendent, becoming assistant superintendent of that line in 1872 and district superintendent in 1873. Ledyard married the daughter of a railroad president and then moved to the Michigan Central to become assistant general superintendent in 1874, general superintendent in 1876, general manager in 1877, president from 1883 to 1905, and chairman from 1905 through 1921, when he died.

An analysis of correspondence by other public relations-minded railroad executives born in the 1830s and 1840s shows that they typically spent their entire careers within the railroad industry and typically argued that whatever was good for the railroad industry was good for America.

For instance, William Ackerman, born in 1832, became assistant secretary and transfer clerk of the Illinois Central at age 20, then secretary of that corporation in 1855, treasurer in 1871, general auditor in 1875, vice president in 1876, and president in 1877. He repeatedly asked for government subsidy of railroads, and was surprised when merchants and other businessmen complained.

Another typical railroad-bred spokesman was Robert Harris. Like Ackerman he joined the industry in 1832 and became superintendent of the Racine and Mississippi in 1856, superintendent of the Buffalo, Baton, Brazos and Colorado in 1860, assistant superintendent of the Chicago, Burlington & Quincy in 1863, general superintendent in 1865, and president in 1878.

Harris became vice-president of the larger Erie railroad in 1880, then president of the Northern Pacific in 1884 and chairman in 1888. He was also a director of the Atchison, Topeka and Santa Fe. He exhibited loyalty not to any particular company but to the railroad industry as a whole. Harris' correspondence is filled with reference not to competition for profit but to two other "P"s: Pooling and public relations.

The economic practice that became known as pooling had two variations. The freight or traffic pool was an anticompetitive agreement allotting a percentage of the traffic within a region to each participating railroad. The typical agreement of that kind would provide that if any road exceeded its "share" of the total business, freight would be diverted from it to other roads until the agreed proportion was established.

The money pool was even more direct: Gross earnings of all collaborating companies would be added up and divided among the collaborators according to fixed percentages. Both types of pools were designed to keep up prices by eliminating rate competition.

Pools became popular during the 1870s. Midwestern railroads developed one in 1870. Eastern railroads adopted rate agreements and a private enforcing commission in 1874. Thirty-two southern railroads agreed on rates and a division of markets in 1875. Seven southwestern railroads established a pool in 1876. Ledyard provided a typical executive view of the activity: "I am a believer in pooling arrangements as being the best method yet devised for preventing undue competition."[8]

Nevertheless, the pools had only brief success, for various reasons. First, as with all cartels from the Tower of Babel to OPEC, differing interests among the participants led to frequent break-ups. In addition, some executives had a nagging sense that collaborative behavior was wrong, and therefore had low resistance to Grangers, merchants, and other groups of rail transport consumers who protested conspiracy on rates.

The development of pooling practices made public relations essential, because pools were lightning rods for criticism. Executives realized that if rates were to be maintained by collaborative means, the anticartel public mood would have to be changed. The defense of pools, syndicates, trusts and holding companies, in a nation brought up on Jeffersonian traditions of decentralized political economy, would not be easy, but public relations-minded railroad executives wrote that it would be possible *if* the press could be brought along. As Ledyard observed, "The newspapers do, to a greater or lesser extent, mold public opinion."[9]

The first blunt step toward using the press for public relations purposes was the straightforward, modest bribe. Payment of fees for favorable newspaper notice—"puffery"—became so common that a Chicago reporter satirized the practice by publishing his rates:

> For the setting forth of virtues (actual or alleged) of presidents, general managers, or directors, $2 per line . . . For complimentary notices of the wives and children of railroad officials, we demand $1.50 per line . . . Poetry will be made to order at $3 per inch of agate measures. We are prepared to supply a fine line of heptameter puffs, also a limited number of sonnets and triolets, in exchange for 1,000 mile tickets. Epic poems, containing descriptions of scenery, dining cars, etc., will be published at special rates.[10]

A more sophisticated method of press agentry involved what was called "deadheading," or the provision of free tickets and "passes." Norfolk and Western vice-president Frederick J. Kimball noted that "giving passes to newspapermen is about the cheapest form of advertising we can get."[11]

Kimball was so successful in this practice that he was commended by his superiors and, for this and other triumphs, made president of the Norfolk and Western from 1883 through 1895. The public rationale he and others offered for deadheading was that reporters had to be free to cover news wherever it happened, and that railroads were acting in the public interest by providing transport.

Using deadhead practices to obtain favorable articles seemed particularly important when the Supreme Court began a practice of examining public opinion (as measured in newspaper articles) before reviewing important cases. In 1876 Ackerman of the Illinois Central wrote to an Iowa public relations agent, J. F. Duncombe, "We cannot afford to remain idle and allow the cities to give the Supreme Court the idea that popular opinion demands" review of a pro-railroad decision. "I want to get your aid by having you publish some articles in the interior of the State commending the decision." These articles could then be produced as evidence of public opinion in the heartland. Duncombe was successful in having articles published throughout Iowa.[12]

Ackerman and his associates began working behind the scenes in other areas as well. Ackerman saw the value of what we now call "educational relations" or "academic affairs," and suggested that many of the ideas that find their way into newspapers originate at colleges and universities. Ackerman argued that escalating public attacks on railroads made it necessary for industry leaders to manufacture public opinion, not just minimize its impact through puffery.

Ackerman delegated his assistants to prowl the academies, with the goal of promoting pro-railroad scholarship that newspapers could then quote. Illinois Central officials sometimes provided encouragement and research help to authors of favorable books and articles, but increasingly provided financial encouragement. By 1880 they were paying for favorable books and articles, which would be published as independent pieces of analysis and scholarship.[13]

A well-rounded strategy required close ties between planted editorials, phony research, and so forth, and behind-the-scenes lobbying efforts. Ackerman, for instance, subsidized publication of articles in an agricultural journal popular in Illinois, the *Prairie Farmer*, and then used those articles in an attempt to convince Illinois legislators that farm sentiment was on his side. But direct legislative bribery also was used. In 1881 Ackerman told William Osborn, one of his company directors, "We have had some bad reports from Springfield. Corrupt demands seem to become contagious, and it will be necessary to spend a little money there."[14]

Other innovative railroad executives expanded the deadheading principle well beyond the press, using it to win influential friends from their various publics. Railroads provided free passes to politicians who had to visit their constituents or take a vacation, clergymen who needed a restful trip to prepare their sermons, and educators who needed a first-hand look at the battlefields they would describe in their classrooms.

John Brisbin, general manager of the Delaware, Lackawanna and Western, wrote that sending a Pennsylvania state senator a pass for his wife was a "good investment." John Denison, secretary and treasurer of the Burlington

and Missouri River in Nebraska, had a pass issued to a Home Missions minister "not because I am in sympathy with the Home Missionary Society, but because . . . we want friends of this sort in Iowa."[15]

Such contributions always carried an implicit *quid pro quo*. For instance,
when Ledyard received a thank-you letter from an Omaha bishop who had
been sent a year's free pass, Ledyard gave the following step-by-step response:

> I am glad to hear you deny the old statement that 'corporations have no souls,'
> and to give credit to the railroad companies for the aid they have contributed in
> promoting the work of Christianity. No one except a railway manager knows
> the constant demands made upon our carrying corporations for transportation
> either free, or at reduced rates, for all classes of men engaged in laboring in be-
> half of their fellows . . .

> Looking at it from a purely business standpoint, you will no doubt agree with
> me, that in the abstract a bishop, a clergyman, or missionary, has no more claim
> or right to travel at reduced rates than a lawyer, a schoolteacher or a merchant
> . . . Now I think my Dear Bishop that the time has come when the railroad
> companies of this country have a right to look to the clergy, and especially to
> those who, by the ruling of Providence, have been called to higher places, for
> some recognition.

> The country as a whole, especially the laboring classes, [opposes railroad
> companies]. Now is it not a matter worthy of your consideration whether the
> church from a high standpoint of right, ought not to use the power delegated to
> her to disabuse the people of these wrong ideas.[16]

Railroad executives such as Ackerman were innovative in their development of the corporate contributions aspect of public relations. During political difficulty Ackerman advised a donation to Illinois Wesleyan University
because it "would doubtless touch the heart of every Methodist Member of
the Legislature."[17]

Ackerman also recommended an Illinois Central "contribution to the yel-
low fever sufferers" because "It will no doubt be of great benefit to us."
Ackerman understood the public relations usefulness of endowing a hospital
bed, as long as a plaque gave credit to Illinois Central: "Unless we can have
this I do not see any particular advantage in making the endowment."[18]

Public relations thinking may have performed its greatest service to
Ledyard, Ackerman, and others when they were challenged within the industry by those committed to intra-industry competition rather than collaboration.

One older generation executive, John Woods Brooks—president of the
Burlington and Missouri River in Nebraska—criticized the new practice of
corporate contributions. In response to a land commissioner asking for con-

tributions to his favorite college, Brooks (sounding very much like Milton Friedman) wrote, "You should bear in mind that our mission is not that of aiding institutions of learning . . . but rather the building of a railroad that shall open a way for developing the resources of the country we traverse, and making it a fit residence for a large and prosperous population."[19]

The younger, public relations-minded executives insisted that they understood the major mission of their business as well as Brooks did, but there was one difference: They believed they would not be able to conduct their businesses without government backing. Robert Harris of the Chicago, Burlington & Quincy, joined with three of the most articulate railroad spokesmen – Charles Francis Adams, Jr., of the Union Pacific, George Blanchard of the Erie, and Chauncey Depew of the New York Central – in puzzling over ways to gain such support and thereby institutionalize collaboration.

Adams, Blanchard, and Depew were public relations experts. Adams, grandson and great-grandson of presidents, brother of historian–philosopher Henry Adams, was called by the *New York Times* "a man who has written and spoken more than any other man on the railroad side [of the regulation question]. He is the ablest man that the corporations have in their service."[20]

George Blanchard, meanwhile, was one of the leading railroad industry contributors of articles to magazines and journals during the 1880s. Chauncey Depew, spokesman for the New York Central during the 1880s, would be both chairman of the New York Central and United States Senator from New York from 1889 through 1911; he was also considered the best after-dinner speaker of his time. Each argued that pools without governmental enforcement tended to fall apart. Each saw that railroads without government oversight were accused of keeping prices too high, for private gain. Each began to see a radical step, federal regulation, as the public relations cure.[21]

Federal regulation of railroads initially was supported by critics of the industry. Small farmers planted seeds of the concept early in the 1870s, and merchants fertilized whenever they could not get special freight rates. For instance, Chicago businessman William H. Beebe told a Senate investigating committee that he did not approve of federal regulation, but *in his particular case* it would be beneficial. Similarly, when Pittsburgh merchants were unable to get a special deal from the railroads, the Pittsburgh Chamber of Commerce called for federal rate regulation.

Federal regulatory plans made little progress, however, until the strange notion of railroads actually benefiting from the regulation demanded by critics began to appear in executive correspondence during the late 1870s. It gained greater currency among executives as new track was laid by "upstarts" between 1879 and 1882: Total mileage increased from 105,000 miles to 141,000 miles during those three years. Some of the new and expanding railroads insisted on competing rather than "playing fair" by pooling.

When the Wabash Railroad cut rates on livestock shipments, and other lines serving Cincinnati, Louisville, and Columbus also ignored pool stipulations, the rate-making system collapsed. Between July and October of 1881, freight rates fell an average of almost 50% nationwide. This was terrible. Something had to be done. What if federal officials sympathetic to the industry would establish rates that all would be compelled to honor?

Involving the government in this way was dramatically opposed to traditional philosophies of competitive enterprise, but those were being jettisoned. Ledyard argued, "Where there are Commissioners to stand between the railroads and the public much dissatisfaction can be avoided . . . "[22]

Similarly, when Ackerman was angered by his rate-cutting competitors, he wrote that, "As many of the Railroad Companies of our country seem incapable of managing their own affairs, it might perhaps be a merciful interposition of the Government to take up this matter. . . . We would not object to the passage of a bill looking to the appointment of a Commission . . ."[23]

The older generation of railroad executives did object. John Murray Forbes, the 72-year-old chairman of the Chicago, Burlington & Quincy, warned CB&Q President Charles Perkins in 1885 that "the evil of Federal management of Railroads cannot be overstated."[24]

Forbes said a regulatory commission eventually would lead to "the worst and most dangerous form of centralization," for "such revolutions don't go backwards, and if once begun I see nothing for it but the absorption of the 120,000 miles of Railroad by Uncle Sam . . . " For years Forbes continued to argue that establishment of a regulatory commission would set a precedent concerning "the right to manage private property by Government Officials," and that the precedent would lead to "infinite mischief."[25]

Which way would the railroad industry go?[26]

CHAPTER THREE

Railroad Executives
and the Interstate
Commerce Commission

With the railroad industry split down the middle, public-relations tendencies were decisive in development of the Interstate Commerce Commission. Robert Harris was the first to provide a succinct rationale for public–private partnership when he argued that competition served "private interests" but public relations demanded "that the wealth and happiness of the whole should be increased – hence I conclude that the policy of the State should be rather to prevent competition than to encourage it."[1]

Harris also introduced another theme salient throughout the past century when he called for reason rather than the marketplace to define economic winners and losers. Harris demanded "*reasonable* compensation to the owners, *reasonable* compensation to the employees, *reasonable* charges to the users. A 'Trinity' that all should be willing to accept." Harris even proposed the mechanism by which reasonableness could be defined: Appointment of a commission with "public representatives."[2]

The politics of the 20th-century have illuminated the problems caused by a stress on economic reasonableness. In the late 19th-century the term was equated with fairness – but, given the stress on self-interest that seems to be part of our human nature, a seller's idea of fairness was often a buyer's conception of highway, or railway, robbery. In the 20th-century, to reduce such conflicts, many societies have handed over the job of price and wage determination to central administrative organs supposedly made up of the best and brightest economic minds. The result of this stress on mind over market has been, more often than not, bottlenecks, dislocation, and other drains on economic efficiency, along with deprivations of economic freedom.

Although much of this experience was still to come, some late 19th-century executives opposed the new faith in "reasonable" governmental commissions. Perkins, for instance, would complain (as the Interstate Commerce Act eventually took shape) that "the power is lodged in the hands of five commissioners . . . It is placing too much power in the hands of five men." Yet, many executives and their Washington lobbyists seemed convinced that the most likely regulatory officials were "just the kind of men we want to study this railroad question instead of leaving it wholly to State politicians . . . " Charles Francis Adams, Jr., wrote that "everything depends upon the men who, so to speak, are inside": A commission filled with the "right men" could fix railroad rate problems.[3]

Still, uncertainty remained. There were no precedents for a federal regulatory commission, and some executives were not eager to buy pigs in pokes. However, the equivalent of today's "issue analysts" examined rate-setting controversies and concluded that there was no alternative to greater governmental involvement in railroad management: "The public will regulate us to some extent . . . " In addition, Ackerman's Illinois Central staff concluded that national control was better than state or local control, because experience had shown that bribed state legislators were untrustworthy: Illinois state senators "will drink all you offer them, and make you any amount of wild promises, but their actions . . . give lie to the promise. In short, they are utterly unreliable."[4]

Pro-regulation executives also buttonholed the uncommitted by developing terminology that has since become standard in campaigns: "public interest," "new ideas," "bipartisanship." Albert Fink, a railroad trade association executive, argued that anticompetitive measures including federal rate setting were "absolutely required for the public interest."[5]

Charles Francis Adams, Jr., further developed the public interest concept by arguing that "a new idea . . . a new phase of representative government" — the regulatory commission — had been made essential by the increasing complexities of industrial technology. Rapid change, according to Adams, required control by a body of dispassionate experts who would use "statistics" rather than emotions or political considerations to harmonize "the interests of the community" with the interests of business.[6]

Executives adept at public relations also designed the strategy that would minimize public opposition to the establishment of a commission. They suggested that public attacks would arise if the railroads seemed to be running the show; therefore, the industry should work behind the scenes: "If the railroads want to try to guide legislation they should do it by agreement with their friends privately . . . " The collaborators' goal was to let sympathetic government officials push the regulatory idea. Joseph Nimmo, Jr., a government statistician, became the front man. Nimmo was able to use a Treasury Department report to propose "a confederation of the railroads under governmental sanction and control, the principle of the apportionment of competitive traffic being recognized as a feature of such a confederation . . . "[7]

Because the railroad executives used front groups and supportive officials in their campaign, some historians have been confused about the impetus for regulation. Grangers and other political groups made noise, but legislation to quiet them was easy; as Adams wrote, it was simple to produce "something having a good sound, but quite harmless, which will impress the popular mind with the idea that a great deal is being done, when, in reality, very little is intended to be done." The real question was not whether Congress would produce radical legislation, but whether Congress, in the words of George Blanchard of the Erie, would give railroads "protection against radical assaults" by reinforcing those "cooperative traffic federations" known as pools.[8]

Some Congressmen were in the railroads' pockets, but others would provide such protection only if they were convinced that unrestrained competition was worse than regulation. Thus the anticompetitive, proregulation thrust of much railroad public relations effort during the key years of 1881 and 1882, when new lines were starting up every month and competition was at its height. Although it is impossible at this point to evaluate with total assurance the effectiveness of this campaign, a reading of 1881-1882 railroad coverage by eight newspapers from around the United States—the *Rocky Mountain News*, the *San Francisco Examiner*, the *New Orleans Picayune*, the *Kaufman (Texas) Sun*, the *Chicago Tribune*, the *Atlanta Constitution*, the *New York Times* and the *New York Tribune*—provides some indication.

These newspapers performed their greatest service to the public relations-minded railroad executives by simply giving front page coverage to their pronouncements. For instance, the *New York Times* had as its lead story on February 26, 1882, an article on "The Railroad Problems. How They Could be Solved by a National Commission." The article reported a speech by Charles Francis Adams, Jr., before the Merchants' Association, an organization of Boston businessmen. Adams frankly acknowledged that his purpose in speaking before the group was to gain "public attention" for his proposal to establish "a Board of Commissioners of inter-State commerce." He succeeded, as his speech was also the lead story in the *New York Tribune* and other newspapers.[9]

The *New York Times* reported that "prominent railroad managers are beginning to look toward legislation as a means of protection," due to "the breakdown of the combination by which rates were maintained and a harmonious working of rival lines secured . . ." The *Times* editorially embraced the collaborative position: The railroad "business cannot be successfully conducted under a system of free competition in which rates would be regulated, like other prices, by the law of supply and demand."[10]

A chief argument of those who wanted the lower freight rates required by competition was that both consumers and producers would benefit from them. It is therefore significant that many newspapers agreed with railroad public relations arguments that middlemen, not producers or consumers, would be the actual beneficiaries of lower rates. The *New York Tribune*, for instance, downplayed the importance of railroad rate competition to consumers and producers by arguing that "The middlemen or traders reap most of the advantage." The *Tribune* also praised one railroad-backed proregulatory pamphlet as "a fresh and interesting contribution to the discussion of the railroad problem," for it emphasized "the evils of excessive competition."[11]

Tribune editors noted that they had benefited from study of the position of "some of the most thoughtful railway managers and students of railways affairs. . . " The railway managers argued "that the prop of some external restraining influence is necessary to insure the maintenance of good faith between the different companies," and the *Tribune* agreed: Railroad-supported governmental regulation was "the only available expedient to this end."[12]

Newspapers from other parts of the United States indicated similar positions. The *Atlanta Constitution* during October, 1881, gave prominent play to a railroad leader's call for establishment of a federal railroad commission. The *Kaufman Sun* called for unconditional backing of railroad industry desires, because it would be wrong to hinder "the goose that lays the golden egg." The *Rocky Mountain News* frequently quoted industry-spokesman Albert Fink on the assured income railroad corporations deserved, due to their wonderful services.[13]

The *Chicago Tribune* ran uncritical articles about, and interviews with, public-relations-minded railroad executives. For instance, in March 1, 1881, railroad executive J. H. Devereaux was given ample space to argue that lowered prices do not benefit the public, and that competition contributes to unfairness. During the following week Erie executive Hugh J. Jewett voiced a similar position in an interview, and other articles explained that railroad companies always had the good of the public in mind.[14]

Later, the *Tribune* ran more interviews with proregulatory railroad executives, along with an essay on "The propriety of regulating commercial intercourse (especially relating to railroads) between the states by National legislation," and an editorial "In Favor of Railroad Commissioners." In reporting falling freight rates, the *Tribune* did not cheer that effect of competition, but contended that, "All rates are badly demoralized and there is no prospect of immediate change." The perspective here is significant: Railroad executives might complain about demoralized rates, but shippers would enjoy bargains.[15]

None of the above necessarily means that railroad executives were controlling or even unduly influencing newspaper editors, who were beset by advocates of all kinds. But those executives who still favored competition saw their position losing out in the public relations war. Forbes, for instance, learned that the major attacks on his antiregulatory position were coming not from Grangers or other antirailroad partisans; no, if he wanted to "uphold private enterprise" he must try to "stop railroad men themselves from advocating government interference in the building of railroads."[16]

Apparently, though, it was too late. When the House of Representatives and then the Senate Committee on Interstate Commerce held hearings in 1884 and 1885, dozens of railroad executives testified in favor of federal involvement. John P. Green, vice-president of the Pennsylvania Railroad, explained that most railroads "would be very glad" to come under Washington's "direct supervision" in return for mandated "rates upon their traffic which would insure them six% dividends."[17]

Significantly, the more astute railroad executives did not walk blindfolded into what would become a regulatory minefield. Chauncey Depew, in advocating the establishment of an Interstate Commerce Commission, showed an understanding of both fundamental problems and short-term business psychology:

> I think I can safely speak for the whole railroad interest of the United States that whatever may be the constitutional objections to the power of Congress, and they are certainly very great, and from the legal side I have grave doubts about it; however, from the practical business side, if there was a national board, with supervisory powers, fully authorized to investigate and report to Congress, I do not believe that there is a railroad, great or small, within the limits of this republic that would ever raise that constitutional question.[18]

Depew was right. The Senate had blocked railroad legislation for almost a decade, but on January 18, 1886, the Senate Committee on Interstate Commerce issued its report:

> The committee has found among the leading representatives of the railroad interests an increasing readiness to accept the aid of Congress in working out the solution of the railroad problem which has obstinately baffled all their efforts, and not a few of the ablest railroad men of the country seem disposed to look to the intervention of Congress as promising to afford the best means of ultimately securing a more equitable and satisfactory adjustment of the relations of the transportation interests to the community than they themselves have been able to bring about.[19]

When the Interstate Commerce Act of 1886 was debated by the whole legislature, warnings were rampant. Senator John T. Morgan of Alabama argued that the Interstate Commerce Commission would have "powers, a large admixture of power, quite a voluminous array of powers. . . . It is the first bill I have ever known to be brought into the Senate . . . where the authors of it were not willing to enter into a definition as to whether the powers they conferred by the bill" were executive, legislative, or judicial. Senator E. C. Walthall of Mississippi opposed establishment of the ICC because of "the fullness of its powers, the disastrous consequences of its mistakes, and the dangers and temptations incident to the position of its members. . . ." Senator George F. Edmunds of Vermont similarly argued that the commissioners would have too much discretionary power.[20]

Some rhetoric in the House of Representatives was harsher. John H. Reagan of Texas argued that, "The American people . . . are not accustomed to the administration of the civil law through bureau orders. This system belongs in fact to despotic governments, not to free republics." Jacob Campbell of Ohio complained that, "This commission, which may be ignorant, willful, or corrupt, [will be] all the while responsible to nobody for their actions."[21]

Railroad public relations assistants, though, were active. William Shinn promoted the legislation through an article in *Railway Review*: Governmental regulation, he argued, could stop "the rate wars which have of late years so devastated the finances of railroad companies . . ." Shinn helped to create a "bandwagon effect" by proclaiming that "the leading railroad companies which formerly (and as I then thought, unwisely) opposed such a commission, are now almost without an exception in its favor."[22]

Another publicist effectively argued in newspapers that "leading railway managers" favored regulation because they had gained humility:

> The irregularities that have gradually crept into [the railroad system] got beyond their capability to manage. . . . The effort to maintain rates was equally unsuccessful. Then came the last resort – the pool – but that, too, proved impotent. . . . Now, acknowledging the inefficiency of their own weak inventions . . . the managers are content to leave the settlement of the whole matter to the law-making power of the country . . . [23]

Based on that rationale, the House and Senate eventually agreed on a bill that established the commission. The Interstate Commerce Act was signed into law by President Grover Cleveland on February 4, 1887.

In the short run, public-relations-minded railroad executives got exactly what they wanted. Thomas Cooley, who advocated the legalization of pooling under governmental control, was appointed chairman of the new Interstate Commerce Commission. Sections of the legislation, which could be troublesome if interpreted harshly by the commissioners, were interpreted in the railroads' favor; for instance, the railroads were allowed to suspend section four, which would not allow them to raise rates for "short hauls," anytime they felt circumstances warranted price increases.[24]

Using the new law as the authority, railroads were able to revamp their freight classifications, raise rates, and eliminate fare reductions. Although the Interstate Commerce Act on paper prohibited pooling, largely as a sop to angry farmers, such a ban made little difference because railroad executives now had something better. In the words of Interstate Commerce Commission member Aldace Walker, "As a prevention of rate wars and destructive competition" the law as interpreted by the commission "is already recognized by intelligent railroad men as better than the pool."[25]

Three conclusions emerge from a study of railroad public relations during the second half of the 19th century. First, railroad executives gained public relations sophistication very fast during the 1870s and 1880s. After an early emphasis on simple press agentry, they began developing the forerunners of today's elaborate governmental relations, educational relations, and corporate contributions programs.

Second, the new public-relations-mindedness was crucial in overcoming traditional principles opposed to governmental involvement. Railroad public relations during the 1880s sold the notion of a federal role in allowing and even promoting collaborationism for the public welfare. Even the Republican Party platform of 1884 contended that, "The principle of public regulation of railroad corporations is a wise and salutary one for the protection of all classes of the people. . . " By 1885, with railroad public relations acquiescence, a general view was becoming popular, according to Lee Benson: "Corporations performing delegated functions of the State, which can only be carried on by exercising a public franchise, must be controlled by the State. . . "[26]

A third perspective, however, is crucial: Although the Interstate Commerce Act enabled railroads to establish the stable rates that they desired, in the long run Cass, Forbes, and others among the older generation of executives proved correct: Federal regulation was the beginning of the end of railroad prosperity, and did the general populace little good either. As Albro Martin noted in *Enterprise Denied: Origins of the Decline of American Railroads, 1897–1917*, railroad leaders eventually realized they had helped to begin a story "of the brutal substitution of a petty consistency for a sensible pragmatism; of the unconscionable elevation, by the government of a republic, of one set of interests over another."[27]

As the membership of the Interstate Commerce Commission became less supportive of railroad executives, and as regulated railroads found less reason to react rapidly to technological change, early warnings about the danger of governmental authority over private enterprise became salient once again. Yet, as the decline in productivity contributed to by public-relations-mindedness became more evident, greater attempts to "keep the public happy" through increased public relations activity (rather than an improved product) became common. Ray Stannard Baker would be able to describe the activities of 43 employees of the Publicity Bureau in Chicago as follows:

To this office comes every publication of any sort within the Chicago territory –
every little village paper in Nebraska, Wisconsin, Illinois, and other states. All
of these are carefully scanned by experienced readers and every article in any
way touching upon the railroad question is clipped out and filed. But the bureau
does not depend upon the papers alone. Traveling agents have visited every
town in the country and have seen, personally, every editor. The record of these
visits is recorded in an extensive card-catalogue. Here is the name of the town;
the name of the editor, the circulation of his paper, whether he is prosperous or
not, his political beliefs, his view on the trust problem, on the liquor question,
even on religious subjects . . . in this catalogue I could almost see the little vil-
lages out in the Mississippi Valley, see the country editor in his small office, and
understand all his hopes, fears, ambitions.[28]

Once the railroads became public-relations-minded, there may have been
no alternative to such operations. As George Washington Cass, Jr., argued,
the pit was bottomless. Cass had a long and happy life, with a successful business career, thirteen children, and a faith in Providence. In 1888, one year
after the Interstate Commerce Commission was signed into law, Cass died.
Although the era of feisty, independent private enterprise that he represented
still had many years to run, advocates of governmental involvement in business activities had taken a major step.

CHAPTER FOUR

Two-Front War:
Early 20th-Century
Utility Public Relations

For the next key development in the growth of large-scale public relations, we turn to the largest telephone and electric utility companies.

First we will see how and why utility leaders responded to early 20th-century muckraking attacks by developing a "two-front war" public relations strategy that opposed not only the left, but smaller competitors as well.[1] Then we will examine some utility public relations techniques, including the use of editorial boilerplate services, the dispatching of managers to become leaders of community groups, the production of ghostwritten articles, and the alteration of school textbooks. Finally, we will examine some of the personal costs involved in selling the concept of "regulated monopoly."[2]

The story of modern utility public relations begins with Samuel Insull, who came to the United States from England in 1881 to be Thomas Edison's secretary, then Edison's key manager and strategic planner. Edison's inventions turned dozens of industries upside down. Insull learned from him how quickly new inventions could alter radically existing patterns of commerce, under conditions of free competition. Insull resolved that when he was in power, competition would not disrupt his plans.[3]

Insull came to the city which he would dominate for four decades when he took control of Chicago Edison in 1892. He learned to play political hardball in one of the nation's major leagues, the Chicago city council. By 1897, Insull had gained enough influence to receive a 50-year electric utility franchise from the council. He also acquired exclusive area rights to buy the electrical equipment of every American manufacturer. This meant that even if someone else could obtain a Chicago franchise, it probably would be worthless.[4]

Once Insull was dominant, he increasingly developed anticompetitive arguments and techniques. As president of the National Electric Light Association (NELA), a major utility trade group, Insull argued that utility monopoly and "franchise security" could best be secured by the establishment of government commissions that would present the appearance of popular control. Insull suggested that the way to sell such a plan to the public would be through emphasis on the commissions' power to fix rates. He told utility owners there was no need to worry about regulation: Regulated rates might be slightly lower than those utility owners would prefer to charge, but they would be higher than what would prevail under full competition.[5]

Insull's long-term goal was to show the public that competition in public utilities was unfeasible. Although most Americans during the past half-century have tended to think of electric utilities as "natural monopolies," recent analysis has shown that there is nothing natural about such status. Poole, Hazlett, Mellor, Allen, and others have shown that competition in provision of electricity leads to lower prices and better service as it has in other areas.[6] Early in this century, at least, it appeared that competition would reign in utilities. Then Insull went to work.

To promote his belief in the uses of government regulation, Insull initially established a NELA committee on Legislative Policy. He appointed to it four men who also opposed competition: Alex Dow of Detroit, Samuel Scovil of Cleveland, H. M. Atkinson of Atlanta, and Ernest H. Davis of Williamsport, Pennsylvania. Insull and the four began giving speeches opposing open competition. They also established advertising and public relations sections in the companies they controlled.

Insull laid down specific rules for utility public relations conduct. First, utility public relations was to heighten fears of socialism in order to promote acceptance of government-regulated monopoly as a less-undesirable alternative. Insull biographer Forrest McDonald has noted that Insull had no objection to socialism in general and "lobbied for twenty years to bring about a government-owned system for England."[7]

Insull would have been able to maintain his power under any system, public or officially private, in which governments afforded his organization monopoly status. But he knew that most Americans favored a competitive system and would support regulated monopolies only if they were seen as preventers of socialism rather than stiflers of competition. "With other men who advocated regulation," Forrest McDonald concluded, "he set out to play upon and aggravate this fear and to pose regulation as the only alternative."[8]

Second, Insull realized that he and his governmental associates would have to perform a charade at times, for those favoring competition would stand for regulated monopoly only if the regulators were seen as severe watchdogs. Insull's principle was never to attack a governmental official who attacked him: "One must expect and accept public denunciations by one's political friends, whenever political expediency necessitated."[9]

Third, Insull believed that industry executives, as soon as the time was right, should lead the fight for increased regulation. Such a stance would allow executives to develop alliances with proregulatory politicians who would man the regulatory commissions when established, or at least appoint their officials. Under Insull's instigation, NELA in 1906 established a Committee on Public Policy which lobbied vigorously for establishment of state regulatory commissions. The NELA convention in 1907 accepted the committee's recommendations, lobbied for increased regulation, and soon had proindustry regulatory boards established in every crucial state. The boards were then able to forestall criticism of utilities by taking symbolic anti-utility actions from time to time.[10]

Similar public relations planning was going on in the telephone industry. Theodore Vail, who had been president of American Bell during the 1880s, rejoined the company in 1902 by becoming a member of the AT&T board of directors. At that time Bell's dominance of the telephone industry could not be taken for granted. In 1903 Bell listed 1,278,000 subscribers. That same year independent companies had over two million.[11]

In 1905 the independents seemed likely to win; an electrical engineer wrote a book on *How the Bell Lost Its Grip*. Vail perceived that the danger to Bell came predominantly from competition, not regulation.[12] Vail resumed the presidency in 1907 and immediately analyzed the Bell System's competitive problems city by city.

The results were troublesome. In Toledo, a Home Telephone Company began competing in 1901 with the local Bell franchisee. Charging rates half those of Bell, it had 10,000 subscribers in 1906, compared to 6,700 for Bell. In Nebraska and Iowa independent phones outnumbered those of Bell 260,000 to 80,000. Cities with referenda on the granting of independent franchises voted decisively in favor of competition rather than regulated monopoly. In Portland, Oregon, a new telephone company won a franchise by a vote of 12,213 to 560. In Omaha the independent company was approved by a vote of 7,653 to 3,625. A national survey of 1,400 businessmen showed 1,245 saying that competition had resulted or could result in better telephone service in their cities, with 982 adding that competition had forced Bell to improve its own service.[13]

Vail observed that Bell was continuing to promote itself on the grounds that only a monopoly system would allow telephone users in different cities or different parts of a town to talk with each other. Yet, Vail knew that system interconnects quickly were becoming technologically feasible. During the

1980s both practice and theory are establishing the logic of competing telephone companies now; they apparently were practical in the early days of telephony as well.[14]

Vail continued and even expanded the natural monopoly theme, but many scoffed. Vail and his key public relations assistant, James Ellsworth, thus developed three additional lines of defense.

Bell's best answer to competition, from the consumer's point of view, was rate-cutting. Cleveland's Bell licensee cut prices from $120 to $72 for a business phone and from $72 to $48 for a home telephone to meet the competition, and other local franchisees took similar steps. But this procedure was costly to Bell, and for that reason generally a last resort.[15]

A more frequent defense was political, when situations were right. In Buffalo, the Bell licensee succeeded in having the city council force the competing Frontier Telephone Company to pay the city $50,000 in cash, give the city free use of 100 telephones, and pay a 3% gross-receipts tax. Bell had no such requirements. Frontier soon went under. But the political shenanigans and occasional payoffs needed to produce such deals could backfire. In San Francisco a Bell licensee vice-president, Louis Grant, was sentenced to five years in prison for attempting to bribe city supervisors.[16]

Bell's third and most important line of defense, once Vail took over, was public relations. Even before Vail came back, AT&T had already gained a reputation for pressure tactics such as the coupling of advertising expenditures with requirements for editorial puffs.[17] But Vail, like Insull, had larger ambitions. His goal was not only to gain a few polite mentions but to win public support for regulatory agencies, which could establish barriers to telephone competition. Vail argued that AT&T could successfully fight the two-front war—stifling smaller companies on one front and holding off the federal government on the other—if it convinced the public that economic efficiency *demanded* one big telephone company.[18]

Vail's conception of the two-front war was apparent in an article he produced for *Atlantic* in 1915 on "Public Utilities and Public Policy." Vail vented less spleen on socialism than on "vicious acts" of competition. For instance, Vail argued that competition creates bad public relations for business, because "The settlements of competitive wars always affect the public unfavorably, not only toward the ones engaged, but toward all other industrial or utility enterprises. When prices are restored . . . they are in constant contrast with the cut price of competitive war, and the consumer is constantly reminded of the differences and resents them . . ."[19]

For Vail, the prime enemy was clear: Competition. He did not like "Competition—excepting that kind which is rather 'participation' than 'competition,' and operates under agreement as to prices or territory . . ." Vail, like Insull, knew that other businessmen as well as the public generally still needed to be convinced about the uses of regulation. "Some corporations have not as yet quite got on to the new order of things," Vail complained, "Relations between the public and the corporations have not fully adjusted themselves to that nicety of balance which is possible, and which will give each of them all that either is entitled to, or could get."[20] To achieve that nicety of balance, a total public relations war would have to be waged.

Early in the century, telephone and utility–industry public relations officials merely followed patterns set by the railroad industry toward the end of the 19th century. They used the railroad technique of paying freelancers to produce favorable articles, without having the economic relationship made public. For instance, George Michaelis of the Boston Publicity Bureau was hired to produce an article in *Moody's Magazine* favorable to utilities, but was identified in the magazine merely as a "writer on economic subjects."[21]

AT&T also adopted several uneconomical practices for public relations purposes. Some lawyers were hired for their expertise, but others for their valuable contacts. Some contacts for supplies were awarded to the highest bidders, in order to make new friends. AT&T paid membership fees and expenses of managers dispatched to join community organizations under orders to socialize with political and civic leaders. But these techniques still seemed somewhat random and incomplete. Vail wanted a company expanding its service into every hamlet to have public relations efforts in every hamlet also. A way to take advantage of the growing national communications networks was needed.[22]

Telephone and utility public relations managers went beyond the railroad model only when they adopted the principle of leaving nothing to chance. The subsidized freelance article or the useful social contact were opportunities to be pursued as they became available, but the goal of 20th-century public relations became the manufacture of new opportunities.

The growth of national magazines and metropolitan newspapers in the 1890s meant that mass communications would become more uniform in the 20th century. The development of the assembly line meant that new production standards were in reach. The telephone and electric utility stress on total, comprehensive public relations coverage was a similar quantitative leap.

Vail and Ellsworth took the first step toward the public relations assembly line when they institutionalized the use of what came to be called "third party" editorial services. AT&T affiliates subsidized and sometimes established services to send out material favorable to Bell's regulated monopoly concept, but without any mention of economic relationship.

Over $100,000 went to E. Hofer and Sons, a firm located in Salem, Oregon, away from major media centers. Annual payments of $84,000 from Insull's NELA allowed Hofer to send out almost 13,000 newspaper articles annually. The articles usually appeared as unattributed, "original" editorials.

Hofer called itself an independent organization unconnected to corporate interests, but the agency received at least half of its income from utilities alone.[23]

Use of such services was only a first step, though. Soon industry front groups began sending out enormous numbers of public relations "news releases." For example, in 1920 and 1921 "five million pieces of literature" were circulated in Illinois alone by the Illinois Committee on Public Utility Information, headed by Insull's top public relations aide, Bernard J. Mullaney. Mullaney deliberately sent newspapers huge amounts of accurate copy to accustom editors to reliance on his work. Only after full trust was established would he begin slipping in a few fast ones. Mullaney noted proudly that his work became most valuable only when saturated editors began lowering their guard. Public relations managers working in other states reported similar successes.[24]

Telephone companies also found this procedure useful. Ohio Bell Telephone Company officials could eventually report that local newspapers, convinced by the initial accuracy of press releases, had stopped sending reporters to rate hearings.[25] Michigan Bell Telephone reported that its publicity hands virtually controlled coverage of the company in that state's newspapers. Evidence made public during FCC and FTC investigations would show how many utility public relations practitioners used initial accuracy to build up trust, in order to take advantage later.[26]

Messages reiterated through this method typically praised governmental regulation of utilities. "Regulation such as we have" is highly desirable, one statement argued, because it "is virtually public ownership." Rates fixed by free market forces may be "incorrect," but "a public utility company's rates are fixed by regulatory authority" so they are "fair."[27]

To make sure these messages were heard, utility public relations men and women were instructed to develop "friendships" with newspaper editors, then exploit them. Electric utility public relations manager George E. Lewis boasted to associates that he had gained "the confidence of hundreds of newspapers in New Mexico, Colorado, and Wyoming" and "the friendship of dozens of editors. It has taken three years of effort to establish this relationship. It will be necessary to capitalize this confidence and friendship during the next few years." He kept a file of letters from editors such as Edwin Bemis, who wrote after attending a utility-sponsored party, "You are creating a wonderful volume of good will . . . Any time you desire any cooperation from the papers which we can give, I hope you will feel free to call on us . . . "[28]

Bell telephone publicists also were told to "go out of your way if necessary to render a service to editors." This generally meant giving editors free long-distance telephone service.[29] But public relations managers were often contemptuous of newspaper editors whose friendship was so forthcoming. J. B. Sheridan, director of the utility-sponsored Missouri Public Relations Committee, wrote that the editors he serviced were useful, but "All of them are 'God's fools,' grateful for the smallest and most insignificant service or courtesy." Sheridan had more respect for those who proceeded on a cash basis. He wrote in 1922, "The time is ripe for getting very close contact with the newspapers. If we can stimulate a little local advertising for some of the leading papers in the state, I think we will have the newspapers and the operators so closely associated that it will be impossible to split them out in the future."[30]

To nail down the frequent use of utility publicity, cash often was needed. As their campaign for total coverage commenced, Insull and Mullaney told associates to "promulgate the idea rapidly among the newspapers that public utilities offer a very fertile field for developing regular, prompt paying, customers of their advertising columns. When that idea penetrates the United States, unless human nature has changed, we will have less trouble with the newspapers than we had in the past."[31]

Guy B. Newburn, director of the Tennessee Public Utility Information Bureau, reported typical success in playing on human nature: Forty Tennessee newspapers ran pro-utility editorials after he placed ads with them. Sheridan of Missouri reported "the splendid effect upon the editors" of increasing advertising: "We now stand very well with the editors, and the press of the State." Editors on the take sometimes demanded more. Editor Charles W. Fear threatened Sheridan, "Have not had any advertising from the Missouri Power and Light Company for two months now . . . I can show up conditions which will look bad if I must. . ."[32] He soon was satisfied.

From the utility perspective, prime placement of material unidentified by source was excellent, but bylined articles by well-known reporters could take advantage of those writers' credibility and thus be even more effective. A ghostwriting industry along these lines soon developed. Newburn of Tennessee sent clippings to C. A. Beasley of the Alabama Power Company and commented, "I want to call your attention particularly to the story appearing in the [Memphis] *Commercial-Appeal,* under the signature of R. M. Gates, Washington correspondent . . . The story which he filed is one which I dictated, and it appeared in the *Commercial Appeal* exactly as dictated to Mr. Gates by me." Leon C. Bradley, director of the Alabama Public Utilities Bureau, reported similar successes. S. E. Boney of the North and South Carolina Bureau wrote an article printed in the Kinston *Free Press* under the byline of editor H. Galt Braxton. The pattern was set.[33]

Mullaney's managers impressively developed roundabout methods of gaining third party endorsements. For instance, Sheridan of Missouri in 1923 had one of his articles printed as an editorial in the small-town Excelsior *Spring Standard,* just so he could "reprint it as a special bulletin, credit the newspaper in which it appeared with it, and distribute it to all newspapers in Missouri. . ." Boney of the Carolina Bureau convinced the North Carolina attorney-general and a prominent South Carolina judge to contribute articles ghostwritten by Boney to a utility-published magazine, *Public Service.* Boney would then send out press releases announcing endorsements from such leaders.[34]

Other local utility public relations managers developed more subtle forms of sweet-talking. H. M. Blain, director of the Louisiana–Mississippi committee, persuaded editors of most of those states' leading newspapers to run a daily column of questions and answers, "Ask Miss Lou." Some questions came from readers, but questions on utility subjects were slipped in and answered by Blain. The substance was similar to that of the utility press releases and ghostwritten editorials: Opposed to governmental takeover of utilities, but sharply pointing out the "inefficiencies" of competition and the need for regulated monopoly.[35]

Vail died in 1920 but his policies continued for a time. Insull continued strong throughout the 1920s. Increasingly during the decade, however, it became apparent that even comprehensive public relations bombarding of the press was not enough to create public confidence in the regulated monopolies. Electric utility public relations counselors argued that "all community elements must be mobilized." J. F. Owens of the NELA public relations executive committee proclaimed his idea, "Through women's clubs and through the cultivation of the women in the women's clubs, we have one of the greatest avenues for the dissemination of correct information relative to the public utility. . . ." Utility companies bought memberships in local clubs for women employees and managers' wives and tried to get them elected to leadership positions.[36]

Some club leaders were purchased outright. Mrs. John D. Sherman, president of the General Federation of Women's Clubs, was paid $600 per month beginning in October, 1926, to "write" articles prepared for her by utility PR men, who would then place them in leading magazines. Women who did not need cash were sometimes thrilled by bylines. Maria Croft Jennings, president of the South Carolina Federation of Women's Clubs, wrote in a letter to Boney of the Carolina Bureau, "The article that you wrote which you so kindly allowed me to sign as my own has seemed to make quite a 'hit.' I appreciate the copies that you sent and am employing the delightful publicity caused by the various papers copying the article, although I feel quite an imposter. . . ."[37]

"Total community coverage" was the goal. E. C. Deal of the Electric Bond and Share Company recommended that the ideal public utility manager "should identify himself with the Boy Scout movement . . . and should encourage some of his lieutenants to become scout executives, scout masters, etc." Sheridan of Missouri dispatched a colleague to investigate the judging of St. Louis high-school debates concerning electric railways; the debates had been won by those critical of the regulated monopoly position, so Sheridan wanted to "ascertain the means employed to initiate, manage and judge these debates in the public schools." The colleague investigated, but reported that judges had merely selected winners who had an "immeasurably greater number of points in the manner of presenting" their arguments.[38]

"If we have any propaganda," Earle W. Hodges, director of the Arkansas Bureau, boasted at NELA's 1923 meeting, "We so conceal or sugar-coat that propaganda with boosting and working for art that it is generously entered into and gotten back of by all of the chambers of commerce, civic clubs, men's and women's organizations over the State." The Wisconsin Utilities Association adopted the sugar-coating approach and printed a song booklet with words such as (to the tune of "Yes, We Have No Bananas") "Yes, we've no excess profits, No overgrown surplus today. We've interest unceasing, And taxes increasing, And all of the help to pay . . . Yes, we've no excess profits, No overgrown surplus today."[39]

Some of the peudo-subliminal methods that were used seem silly, but orders to produce total coverage led to reports such as that in 1924 by P. S. Arkwright, chairman of the Southeastern Division of NELA. He and his assistants, Arkwright said, placed posters in hundreds of schools. The posters provided "facts about the State, but never any propaganda about the company. This company believes the result is that school children constantly seeing the name of the company associated with facts about the State's greatness are beginning to associate the company itself with the progress of the State."[40]

Some utility public relations officials, believing it was Insull's objective to achieve total communications and educational dominance, moved to excise from government and economics textbooks passages opposing regulated monopoly. This was to proceed secretly, one utilities executive noted, because "if the public were to get the idea that textbooks were being used for propaganda for public-utility companies the reaction would be worse than the original misinformation."[41]

Willing professors were used as spear-carriers. For instance, Horace M. Davis, director of the Nebraska Committee on Public Utility Information, noted in 1925 how he had won support for the regulated monopoly concept:

> We have been at it for more than two years here . . . first selling the idea to the agricultural college folk and letting them take the spotlight and assume all the leadership. Just yesterday we went through the motions of setting up an actual joint committee on relations of electricity to agriculture. The dean of the agricultural college will be chairman but will do little actual work . . . . The college can say things that we can not say and be believed.[42]

Even in 1920 news about the utilities' comprehensive public relations programs was leaking out. As late as 1925, though, journalists did not want to or did not know how to cover the story of utility public relations. Even leading business magazines were sometimes taken in. In 1925, the Alabama Power Company received a silver cup for public relations accomplishment from *Forbes* magazine. *Forbes*, noting that 90% of Alabama newspapers were editorializing favorably about the company, presented a list of company accomplishments that had improved its popularity. Perhaps the improvement was real, but the measurement was faulty: The editorials were canned and shipped from Oregon by Hofer. The newspapers were paid for running them.[43]

Concern about eventual exposure did cause AT&T public relations executives to back away from some NELA schemes. J. L. Spellman, publicity manager of Illinois Bell, served on a committee to force textbook changes but wrote in 1925 that "this whole matter is full of dynamite. Unless it is handled tactfully and intelligently, considerable trouble is bound to result. If anything of a 'brass band' nature is attempted, we immediately lay ourselves open to a charge of seeking to control the material used in the schools."[44] By 1928, when investigations of utility industry public relations began, AT&T was moving away from the Vail–Ellsworth legacy and embarking on a modified course under Arthur Page, the company's new vice-president for publicity and information.

The 1928 investigations were demanded by several angry legislators, but they were aided and advised by utility public relations managers who saw themselves as sorcerer's apprentices careening out of control in an Insull-conceived musical score. Sheridan of Missouri, who had pressured editors and checked high-school debate judges for evidence of anti-utility conspiracy, decided in 1927 that enough was enough. He crossed over by writing, "What can we do when the financiers will inflate, overcapitalize, sell securities based on blue sky or hot air, and rates must be kept up to pay returns on said blue sky and hot air? The best public-relations stuff in the world is a nice little reduction of rates. Do we get it? We do not. I know places where I believe a 13-cent top rate should be 8 cents," but the "monopoly feature" prevents this.[45]

Sheridan suggested that the "remedy" was to "hang the offenders high as Haman upon the gibbet of publicity."[46] That is what the FTC and FCC investigations did, beginning in 1928. Memos and plans quoted in this chapter, and many others, were subpoenaed and made public then. Some individuals were disgraced. After the stock market crash the following year, Insull's empire crashed also, and evidence of security-selling based on deliberate blue sky and hot air was made public. Insull left the United States but was extradited from Turkey and brought back to Chicago for trial, then jail.

Sheridan's views were shared by at least one of his public relations associates, John Colton. Colton wrote to Sheridan:

Just at present I feel very much disillusioned . . . You are absolutely right when you ask the question, as it was asked 2,000 years ago, 'What profiteth it for a man to gain the whole world if he loses his own soul?' The man who cannot look himself in the eye when he shaves himself in the morning, or who hangs his head in the solitude of his bedroom when attempting to address himself to God, is one of the poorest and most miserable creatures, though he have wealth incalculable.

I know that all things work for good, and that seeming defeats may be merely heralds of victory . . . Here's wishing you the best of all good things and assuring you of my sincere friendship.[47]

Sheridan wrote back that in five years of utility public relations "I held my tongue. Now I mean to resume the greatest of human rights—that of free speech." But for Sheridan, in his own mind, it apparently was too late. As governmental investigations continued in April, 1930, he committed suicide.[48]

CHAPTER FIVE

Minimizing Competition
Through Public Relations:
The Work of Ivy Lee

We have now seen how public-relations-minded railroad executives developed anticompetitive rationales during the late 19th century. We have seen how specialized utility public-relations staffers, along with ideologically-motivated opponents of private enterprise, helped to spread the concept across the country early in the 20th century.

With all that pushing, though, managers in many industries during the preDepression days still retained an old-fashioned belief in the virtues of competition. To sell them as well as the public on the virtues of industrial "harmony," some corporate executives hired a man who has become known as the founder of modern public relations – Ivy Lee.[1]

The Lee revealed by some research and hard questioning, though, is not the Lee treated as a patron saint of private enterprise in the opening chapters of standard public relations textbooks. Actually, as we will see in this chapter, Lee worked hard to convince other business leaders and the public that a demise of competitive enterprise was both inevitable and socially useful.

Lee's sophisticated understanding of both economics and popular psychology allowed him to choose facts artfully while twisting interpretation, and in that way cover machinations with talk of cooperation in the public interest. He anticipated modern talk of corporate "social responsibility," and even implied that businessmen who emphasize competition do not love their neighbors and are only out for a buck.

Lee's capacity for innovation made him a puzzle to some. His bold proclamations of integrity – "All our work is done in the open" – were contradicted by actions that won him the sobriquet "Poison Ivy." A friendly *New York*

World reporter asked about Lee, "Why is it then that this amiable gentleman, who provides so many good stories, is so generally disliked by newspaper men?"[2]

Even Lee's supporters were surprised when the "defender of capitalism" wrote a book filled with sympathy for Stalin. But the apparent contradictions were all related to Lee's consistent opposition to competitive enterprise and espousal of corporate collaborationism, that is, alliances of large corporations with each other and with the federal government. Lee's role becomes clear when we examine the way he integrated three major trends in political economy.[3]

First, in 1900 and thereafter, industrial leaders such as J. P. Morgan and John D. Rockefeller were emphasizing consolidation rather than competition. They could look back on a dizzying period of national economic improvement because from 1865 to 1900 U.S. output increased threefold. This was real growth, for deflation dominated prices during the postbellum third of a century. But it was not always easy growth; economic winners and losers abounded.

The winners, who generally had triumphed through innovation and intense competition, knew how easy it was to be toppled, or to at least suffer falling prices and declining profits. They tried to develop price and marketing agreements to give themselves a guaranteed rate of return, but agreements of that sort always seemed to fall through. New technologies, new sources of investment capital, new methods of transportation and communication, rapidly expanding markets due to massive population increases, and easy entry into most of those markets, made anticompetitive agreements short-lived.[4]

Second, as anticompetitive agreements fell through, some industrial leaders began to see federal intervention and regulation as the way to make them stand up.[5] Rockefeller and H. H. Rogers of Standard Oil joined with groups such as the Association of Manufacturers and Distributors of Food Products in calling for national incorporation laws and national regulations that would help them keep out competition by raising barriers to entry.[6]

Federal regulation, according to Daniel Willard, president of the Baltimore and Ohio, could "so harmonize all . . . conflicting interests that, in the long run, the greatest good may come to the greatest number."[7] In 1901, railroad executive James J. Hill spoke of the need to "obviate ruinous competition."[8] James Logan of the American Envelope Co. argued that competition must be controlled because it "means death to some of the combatants. . ."[9] An American Tobacco Co. official believed that the federal presence could help corporations engage in "rational cooperation in lieu of cut-throat competition."[10]

Third, the public generally did not support notions of federally-imposed harmony. Research during the past two decades is correcting previous historians' assumptions that when populists and small business progressives criticized the trusts, they were calling for socialism in some form. Many groups were dissatisfied with trust-building activities because they did not want to have to play politics to get their goods to market. Small merchants shipping goods by railroad, for instance, just wanted equal rates, and not rebates to the favored few.[11]

Those corporate leaders who desired governmental protection, therefore, had a problem: How could a pro-competitive enterprise populace be led to acceptance of the new concept of government-business "partnership"? There is evidence that leaders such as Morgan were true believers in the need to establish a new economic order. They brought out statistics attempting to prove (with some justification) that trusts backed by governments could produce many goods more efficiently than could a variety of small and mid-sized competitors. But the public was not buying. Deep-rooted feelings about liberty and competition could not be budged through economic argumentation.

Leading supporters of "partnership" looked for different means of persuasion. They needed a strategist, one with a sophisticated understanding of both economics and popular psychology. They needed a spokesman who could create the impression that "selling to the public" was inferior to "serving the public interest." They needed someone who could stride into board rooms and convince businessmen committed to selling that a new style of assessing corporate conduct—not just good sales but good "public relations"—was needed.

That someone was Ivy Lee. Lee's years in college and as a young professional were part of the greatest era of trust-building yet seen. From 1895 to 1904 over 3000 companies disappeared into mergers. Lee, top economics student in the Princeton class of 1898, saw what was going on. His yearbook said of Lee, "What he doesn't know about trusts is not worth knowing."[12] Lee's economic thinking was firmly in the collaborationist camp. Capitalism, he would note, "had advanced faster than the ability of the human intelligence to cope with it." Lee argued that "restrictions must be placed on the use of capital so as to obtain, at the same time, the utmost good for the community as a whole."[13]

Lee never defined the "utmost good" or said who would define it, but such a notion had become common at Princeton as the Germanic, positive notion of state power was taking root. Lee even brought himself to write an article explicitly titled *Coordinating Business Through Co-operation*. In it he opposed traditional competition and urged "cooperation" through industrial institutes and trade associations.

Crucially, Lee understood not only the new political economy but the practical political and psychological steps that would have to be taken along the way. He knew that the new collaborationism could be put into place only if businessmen were fully united behind it. That could happen only if businessmen saw collaboration as an inevitable development to which their enterprises must bend in order to avoid breaking.

To convince skeptical businessmen, regulation would have to be packaged as something that could increase economic liberty rather than stifle it. A public relations counselor would also have to convince businessmen that it was improper simply to think of companies responding to customer desires as expressed in the marketplace. He would have to convince waverers that special investigation of public needs was required, with the goal of *administering* rather than selling to markets.

On the surface, such an approach was not particularly sensible. Experienced businessmen trust the person who has to make a sale, not the one who can act any way he chooses and still do well economically. They expect better results from the person who has to fulfill a contract rather than the person who may simply feel like being nice. The concept that "public-relations-mindedness" would be an improvement on the old-fashioned hard-headed desire to sell a product would ordinarily have been laughed at. But Lee had an ace hidden: He added to his economic studies an awareness of currents in popular theology.

Lee, son of a minister who preached a liberalized Protestantism, grew up with social gospel ideas that man could create heaven on earth by establishing a new, "cooperative" social order. Lee was further exposed to new thought at Princeton, where Darwinian ideas were applied to economic trends to show (supposedly) that movement toward larger economic units, and perhaps eventually one state economy, was a movement of inevitable economic progress. As Charles Francis Adams, Jr., had said, "The principle of consolidation . . . is a necessity—a natural law of growth." Competition must be followed by combination, for "The law is invariable. It knows no exceptions."[14]

Lee maintained an interest in theological questions throughout his career. He became a strong partisan of modernism in Christianity. He personally paid for the printing and nationwide distribution of one of the crucial sermons in American ecclesiastical history, Harry Emerson Fosdick's "Shall the Fundamentalists Win?" Fosdick, an early proponent of situation ethics, later said his sermon opposing orthodox Christianity would have had "no unusual result if it had not been for Ivy Lee."[15]

Lee used all his public relations skills to make Fosdick and his beliefs famous and influential. Lee and others even urged John D. Rockefeller Jr. to contribute $26 million toward construction of a new church to house Fosdick, who resigned under fire from his old ministry. Rockefeller did.

Lee also put his theology to immediate professional use as he examined the crucial question of how to sell collaborationism to competition-oriented businessmen and to the general public. He argued that competition was unChristian. He suggested that businessmen who emphasized competition did not love their neighbors but were only out to make a buck. He argued that creation of government-backed cartels would lead to better care for the public because naturally good-hearted businessmen would be able to follow their better instincts instead of acting under pressure for short-term sales.[16]

Lee was able to utter such statements with a straight face for two reasons. First, he showed no understanding of the orthodox Christian concept of original sin. He apparently had come to believe that environmental factors were more essential than natural disabilities in determining conduct. If the business environment were changed, covetousness would give way to kindness. Second, he held to a sub-Christian standard of ethics: While it was improper to lie, he thought neither the Bible nor anything else provided a truly objective standard of judging human activities, so all analyses were essentially subjective.

Lee, combining an emphasis on subjectivity with what he had read from popularized Freudian psychology, arrived at a strategy that he termed the "psychology of the multitude." Give up attempts to explain economic laws through rational discourse, he advised businessmen, for people "will not analyze statistics . . . Since crowds do not reason, they can only be organized and stimulated through symbols and phrases." Communication proceeded better when public relations spokesmen played on "the imagination or emotion of the public. . ." Those favoring collaboration merely had to find "leaders who can fertilize the imagination and organize the will of the crowd . . . the crowd craves leadership."[17]

Lee made a career of telling leaders of the new economic order how to merge the new economics with the new psychology. He told a group of railroad managers that "Crowds are led by symbols and phrases. Success in dealing with crowds . . . rests upon the art of getting believed in. We know that Henry the Eighth by his obsequious deference to the forms of the law was able to get the people to believe in him so completely that he was able to do almost anything with them." Appearances, Lee argued, were the base on which a superstructure of reality could be erected.[18]

In short, Lee understood in 1917 what Lenin was putting into practice, what Joseph Goebbels would refine in the 1930s, and what Jacques Ellul would criticize in the 1950s—the idea that "In propaganda, truth pays off." As Ellul concluded, ". . . in propaganda we must make a radical distinction between a fact on the one hand and intentions or interpretations on the other; in brief, between the material and the moral elements. The truth that pays off is in the realm of facts. The necessary falsehoods, which also pay off, are in the realm of *intentions* and *interpretations*."[19]

Lee's tactic of factual accuracy in order to insinuate impressions was far more effective than the policy of J. P. Morgan, who generally did not allow his conclusions to outrun his factual base. It was also a departure from the typical press agent policy of outlandish statements. Lee found the appearance of truthfulness to be as useful to him as it had been in the days of Henry VIII. Listeners who believed him on small points, for good reason, were more likely to follow him to his collaborationist conclusions.

Editors who scorned press agents listened to Lee. By covering machinations with talk of cooperation in the public interest, Lee's clients escaped criticism they might otherwise have received. Lee's thinking went into, and preserved from substantial criticism, the Copper and Brass Research Association; it became the organization devoted to pooling resources to control markets for 42 of the largest copper producers and manufacturers in the United States.

Lee also sold to the public the anticompetitive plans of the Anthracite Coal Operators Conference, composed of 102 companies, saying that the barriers to entry established by the Conference would be a means of preventing adulterated product. Lee worked with lawyer Thomas Chadbourne to establish the International Sugar Council, which developed a plan in 1930 to cut out competition in order to stabilize sugar prices. "Laissez faire" competition, Lee argued, "may mean ruin to large numbers. . ."[20]

Whenever those favoring competitive enterprise criticized Lee's efforts, he created a smokescreen. When criticized for his role in formation of the Cotton Yarn Association, Lee acknowledged that the objective was "establishment of a protective minimum price, trusting thereby to deal with the surplus capacity of the trade and eliminate those sellers of yarn in the market who, by force of circumstances, have been obliged to dispose of their output without reference to price."[21] It would take a moment to cut through such rhetoric to see that the Association's mission was to clamp down on discount sellers. In the meantime, Lee would have moved on.

During the 1920s in particular, Lee spent much of his time trying to convince corporations to establish public relations programs of their own. To promote public relations, Lee enlisted in the drive his close business associates, such as Dwight Morrow of J. P. Morgan, Otto Kahn of Kuhn-Loeb, and Winthrop Aldrich of Chase National. Lee's mission for these and others was not so much to sell the public on business as to sell public relations to business.

Seeing Lee as a proponent of collaboration rather than competitive enterprise, and as a person who combined the new economic thinking with an ethic of fact accuracy but impression manipulation, clears up part of what has been the mystery of Ivy Lee. For instance, we can now reassess his famous Declaration of Principles. Yes, Lee claimed that all his work was done in the open, but at the time he made that pronouncement Lee was employed by International Harvester to write an article for *Moody's Magazine*. The article would praise Harvester as "An Open and Above-Board Trust."[22] Lee would not be identified as a company spokesman. In 1907, when Lee wrote a *Moody's Magazine* article on behalf of his new employer, the Pennsylvania Railroad, his corporate connection once again was not mentioned.[23]

Did such behavior mean that all of Lee's work was not done in the open? No, his Declaration of Principles was factually accurate: The articles were published and his name was on them. But Lee's declaration created an inaccurate impression of a willingness to lay his cards on the table. This he did not do except under pressure. He continued to abide by the letter of his accuracy law, but not the spirit of truth-telling.

A close look at the Declaration of Principles shows how artfully Lee chose his words. For instance, "I send out only matter every detail of which I am willing to assist any editor in verifying for himself."[24] Such a statement was factually correct in that all of Lee's details were generally verifiable, but Lee knew that effective propaganda contains in it only information that can be verified. Lee's goals was to slant his readers and clients toward anticompetitive policies, but so subtly that he would leave with them a belief that they had made up their own minds.

A view of Lee as master propagandist (but not a liar by his own "situation ethic" standards) makes what seem to be mistakes and anomalies part of this newly understood pattern. For instance, Lee was employed by John D. Rockefeller, Jr. to repair damage caused to business-government collaboration by press coverage of the 1914 "Ludlow Massacre." This tragedy was the culmination of a coal miners' strike in Colorado which led to considerable violence, including an April 20 battle between strikers and the Colorado State Militia in which two women and eleven children at Ludlow were killed.

Lee ascertained that the women and children, while fleeing in panic from an out-of-control militia outfit, had overturned a stove and set off the fatal fire in which most of them died. Lee could therefore suggest, in a bulletin sent to newspaper editors, that the women and children may have been the victims of their own carelessness. Some reporters, of course, pointed out the foolishness of expecting persons fleeing in panic to watch their step, and cursed Lee as a Pharisee. But he could state with accuracy that he had not lied.

Lee became adept at creating dishonest impressions from factual statements. In his post-Ludlow cleanup, Lee circulated a bulletin, "How Colorado Editors View the Strike," which contained statements made at a conference of Colorado editors. Judging from the bulletin, the editors were surprisingly supportive of coal company interests. What went unmentioned in the bulletin was that of 331 newspaper editors in the state, only fourteen attended the conference and only eleven signed the report. All eleven were from papers controlled by the coal companies.[25]

The view of Lee as an advocate of collaboration rather than competition clears up other mysteries, such as Lee's relations with, and book promoting, the Soviet Union. In 1930 *Business Week* was astounded when Lee became so great a defender of the Soviet Union that some said he must be a paid agent. "In instinct, doctrine, career," *Business Week* noted, Lee was "the subtlest of protectors of capitalists, their arch advocate, the veritable high priest of their whole controversial business – a professional director of public relations. That he of all men [should support Soviet objectives] is the anomaly, enigma, and mystery of cynical Wall Street."[26] C. W. Barron, editor of the *Wall Street Journal*, asked Lee directly, "What are you doing all this for? Who is paying you for it?"[27]

Lee said the Soviet connection was his hobby, yet *Business Week* sniffed, "Sophisticated managing editors frankly do not believe a word of it. It is simply impossible that Ivy Lee, aide to millionaires and millionairedom, should be serious in all this stuff about Soviet Russia. What a colossal axe he must be grinding."[28] Speculation about Soviet payments to Lee was rampant, but one letter purportedly showing a payoff proved a forgery, and nothing ever has been proven.

Whether or not money was a bond, though, mind apparently was. When Lincoln Steffens toured the Soviet Union, he thought he was seeing the future in a society based on collaborationism taken to its extremes. Lee may not have gone so far, but he did see the United States moving closer to the Soviet Union in social perspective. "The United States started with complete individualism, every man for himself," and the Soviets have the opposite position, Lee wrote, but "we have found it necessary to restrict the power of the individual. . ."[29]

As the two countries' political futures converged, Lee expected that the economic possibilities also would become apparent: "Within five years Russia will have the biggest tractor plant, the biggest paper mills, the biggest of many other industries in the world."[30] Lee's belief in domestic collaboration could easily extend itself into proclamations of the beauty of a United States–Soviet deal. He practiced what he preached by advising Standard Oil and Vacuum Oil to buy Soviet petroleum and also offer loans to the Soviet government.

The *New York Times* reported that deal in March, 1926, and noted Lee's participation, observing that "the best known and most expensive of publicity agents, who among other activities is the advisor on public relations to the Standard Oil interests, has begun to display keen interest in the recognition of the Soviet government." The *Times* also reported that Lee had sent letters to many of his associates urging closer contacts with the Soviets. Editors noted the cooperation of Lee and Ruth Stout, editor of the communist magazine *The New Masses*.[31]

Lee was widely criticized for his Soviet-related activities. Elihu Root asked Lee if he wanted Americans to "accept the principles of the Bolsheviki as something equally as good" as the principles of competitive enterprise.[32] Representative Hamilton Fish, Jr. proclaimed Lee a "notorious propagandist for Soviet Russia."[33] In 1929 Representative George Tinkham of Massachusetts called Lee an "open propagandist" against American interests, with "no country, no flag, aand no allegiance except the power of money, and what money can compel or buy."[34]

That was not true. Lee was consistent in his embrace of government-industry "partnerships" both at home and abroad. He was also consistent in his use of factual accuracy to more effectively mold perceptions. Throughout his career Lee attempted to find or develop economic leaders, whether corporate or Soviet, in whom the crowd could be made to believe. He opposed economic competition, preferring organizations as monopolistic as could be obtained within each economic system. In short, Lee liked "czars" and did not like truly private enterprise.

In 1929, at age 52, Lee looked back on his career and indicated satisfaction at his accomplishments in affecting American political and economy thinking, but concern about the personal cost. He wrote to a friend, "A good many years ago I started on the work I am doing, feeling that there was a real field in it for usefulness. I know now that there is a great deal to be done that is useful . . . [But I have found] the greatest difficulty in getting people to take anything I say as an independent expression of opinion. I am always merely a propagandist . . . Sometimes in my low moments I have thought of throwing the whole thing overboard and taking a minor job as a newspaper editor."[35]

Lee, of course, never did. He succeeded in making the concept of collaboration welcome in many corporations. He seeded some of the largest with public relations counselors. He was the perfect representative for major corporate clients whose goal was to sell the concept of reducing competition "in the public interest." Lee had to be satisfied with that. Advising the executive board of the Pennsylvania Railroad in October, 1934, he suddenly could not remember to whom he was speaking. The diagnosis was cerebral hemorrhage. One month later, at age 57, Lee died.

CHAPTER SIX

The Movie Industry
Gets a Czar:
1921–1934

As we saw in chapter five, one of Ivy Lee's chief recommendations was: When in doubt, find a "czar," someone the public will think is taking charge and personally "cleaning up the mess." The movie industry tried to put his suggestions into effect during the 1920s.[1]

In 1921 the industry needed urgent help because the Roscoe "Fatty" Arbuckle murder case was in the headlines. Arbuckle, a comedian once almost as popular as Charlie Chaplin, was accused of killing actress Virginia Rappe during a Labor Day weekend party. Other crimes, including the murder of director William Desmond Taylor, also caused tongues to wag, not only in courtrooms but in barbershops and legislatures as well. The sensational trial news seemed to confirm what civic and religious groups had been saying about the "Hollywood Babylon" during previous years. "Glorification of adultery," "attack on family values," "relying on sex and violence," were some of the charges thrown at movie studios.

The question for critics of Hollywood was, what to do? Two avenues of approach were taken. First, community groups threatened boycotts of theaters, combined with picketing. Voluntaristic action of that sort, from colonial days onward, was an American tradition, one that allowed purveyors of disliked material the choice of standing fast or abandoning their projects; boycotts, in that they did not involve governmental sanctions, were fully consistent with libertarian theory. Second, though, came the threat of film censorship bills, discussed in many states and passed in some.[2]

Meeting in New York, movie industry heads decided they could shrug off boycott threats and fight off the censorship bills. What made them most uncomfortable were politicians' calls to remove governmental protection from powerful studios and leave them liable to the same antitrust action most industries faced.

Industry leaders had been protected as they had gained control over local theaters through practices such as "block booking," wherein theater owners had to take a studio's entire production, sight unseen, whether they wanted it or not. Block-booking agreements forced on local theater owners under threat of being run out of business were highly anticompetitive, in that they gave certain studios protected monopolies within particular cities or parts of cities. Leading producers decided they could maintain their local monopolies by following public relations recommendations and hiring a front for their operation.[3]

The industry leaders went after Harding administration Postmaster General Will Hays. Hays had the right personal credentials to satisfy dissident groups: He was a Presbyterian church elder for an industry dominated by Jewish producers, a teetotaler in a town with the reputation for wild parties, and a former Republican National Committee chairman who would be useful when problems might require political fixing.[4] Hays, exuding perpetual happiness, also seemed to believe in the good will of everyone he met. As Washington reporter Edmund G. Lowry wrote in one of his Harding administration profiles, Hays:

> is a human flivver . . . an articulate emotionalist if ever there was one; a politician to his fingertips and a strong josher; a real handshaker and elbow massager. He is the English sparrow of the Harding administration: chipper, confident, unafraid, friendly. And he behaves as such . . .[5]

Producers Lewis J. Selznick and Saul Rogers pitched the industry's proposal to Hays on December 8, 1921: "Czar" status and a salary of $100,000 per year. On January 14, 1922, Hays accepted the offer, apparently without a careful examination of the actual powers he would have. For instance, he would "head" an organization to be called the Motion Picture Producers and Distributors of America (MPPDA), although the bylaws merely defined his job as that of "spokesman" for the industry in all communications to the public.[6]

MPPDA directors gave Hays the power to veto actions taken by the board of directors of the MPPDA, subject to overriding by a two-thirds vote, but Hays could not take any actions himself without approval by the producers. Hays, according to biographer Raymond Moley, saw himself not as czar but as "Caesar's slave," and that was what he became.[7]

Hays was also called "the cat's whiskers," due to behavior so ebullient that it often seemed naive. For instance, Hays himself provided a mouth-agape account of his reception at the Hollywood dream factory:

The streets were decorated with bunting and flags and big signs reading WEL-
COME WILL HAYS!. . . . At the Fox lot I was genuinely affected by the warmth
of the greeting accorded me . . . I knew that my reception here as at the other
studios was sincere – the closing down of the sets, celebrities and assistants
swarming out to the specially rigged platform in the sunshine, smiling as warmly
as the sun itself . . . The week ended in a blaze of glory with a mammoth all-
industry rally at the Hollywood Bowl . . . everything went like clockwork. All
the studios shut down at noon, and the personnel of each marched in a body to
the great Bowl, many of the players in the costumes of the productions they
were currently making. It was a riot of color, yet it all blended into a harmonious
pattern on that glorious, cloudless summer day . . . there were at least five thousand columns of favorable publicity covering the events of the week . . . [8]

The whole point was publicity – "Hollywood Cleans Up" – without change
in performance, and a brainwashing of Hays to boot, but Hays' perpetual
trust meant that he could be readily hornswoggled. Hays wrote, "I firmly believe that a sense of right and wrong is implanted in the heart of every human
being not an imbecile and over the age of six. . ."[9] Thus, when producers refused to make substantive changes, Hays would tell industry critics that the
producers had just forgotten what was wanted. "They were sincere," he said
with a smile, "but so are those who make New Year's resolutions. We cannot
find fault if a highly complex subject is not learned overnight." For Hays,
"learning" always was delayed by inability, not by lack of will.[10]

The result of this presuppositional lack of perception was that Hays was
perfect for public relations: He did not even know he was being used. Three
months after his appointment, Hays met with leaders of 60 public service organizations and told them he was on their side. He gave speeches such as "The
Voice of a Free People" in which he insisted that there was nothing to fear but
horror movies themselves.[11]

While Hays was fronting, his associates were instructing studio publicists
to emphasize the wholesomeness of stars and cover up some of their expensive
habits. Bribed writers were told to produce smiling copy. As Terry Ramsaye
reported,

The motion picture industry began to scream with outraged innocence . . .
Writers, better known for their fictional contributions to the scenario departments than for their abilities as reporters, were brought in as a defensive army.
They reached Hollywood in the morning, and by night completed profound articles stating they had been unable to verify reports of wickedness.[12]

Organizationally, the producers established a public relations committee
in 1922 and turned it into a MPPDA Public Relations Department in 1925,
with the appropriately-named Jason Joy as departmental director. The committee in action, though, was less impressive than it appeared on the elabo-

rate organization charts sent out to leaders of community groups who had been criticizing the movie industry.[13]

What those community groups were demanding initially in the 1920s was not much: They hoped that some stars would be good role models for their children, and they hoped that some movies would reaffirm rather than attack their religious and social values. Hays, promising that their requests would be met, introduced in 1924 what he called the "Formula," a vague declaration that studios would reach for "the highest possible moral and artistic standards of motion picture production." But those words proved meaningless.[14]

By 1929 it was clear that Hays' attempts to make producers more conscious of community pressure were not working. Hays acknowledged that "less than half of the member companies of the West Coast Association were making an effort at cooperation."[15] Jason Joy was discouraged, but not Hays: "I refused to be disheartened and I begged Colonel Joy to hang on."[16] Hays pressed on with his faith in words based on good faith; he worked with his friend Martin Quigley, trade-magazine publisher, to develop a Motion Picture Code. When adopted in 1930 by the West Coast Board of Directors and the Motion Picture Producers and Distributors of America, the code gave the Hays organization more power—on paper.

Some of the provisions were onerous. Under the Code, every MPPDA member company had to submit all its films to the MPPDA studio-relations committee. If that committee informed the movie's production manager that the film contained Code violations, the producer was required not to release the film until changes were made.[17] Quigley argued—and Hays, perhaps learning, agreed—that such procedures would be necessary to forestall boycotts by community groups.

The Code procedures quickly became farcical. The individual producer was allowed to appeal decisions to a jury of three members of the MPPDA production committee, which was made up of 17 studio executives (one from each of the member companies). The rotating jury of three, known as the Hollywood Jury, was invariably sympathetic to the producers:

> It made its judgments wholly without objectivity. Colonel Joy lost every appeal . . . Each time this happened, the committee's usefulness was impaired, for the failure of the juries to sustain its contentions was, of course, common gossip in the studios.[18]

After a while, Joy got the point and stopped fighting; if he took a tough stand, it would be overridden by an appeals board made up of logrolling studio executives. As one observer sympathetic to the movie industry noted, "a substantial number of producers never would take the code seriously."[19]

The record of films produced provides additional evidence of noncompliance. Although the Code's goal was to avoid pressures for increased governmental censorship, the New York City censor estimated that, "during the first six months of 1931, the amount of cutting and elimination required [by the New York censorship office] substantially exceeded that of the six months of the year preceding the adoption of the code." Industry public relations was starting to make governmental censors more suspicious rather than less.[20]

The industry kept insisting that it was producing "profamily" movies, but movie magazine publisher Martin Quigley, in a small book entitled *Decency in Motion Pictures*, was specific about the industry's "failure" to keep its pledge.[21] For instance, Quigly criticized the movie "Animal Kingdom" because it is:

A triangle story with the wife the unsympathetic angle . . . The unfolding of the narrative leads the husband to resume a pre-marriage liason eventually, with heroic speeches, leaving the wife and going with the mistress . . . It glorifies and justifies adultery, presenting an extramarital relationship as something pure and heroic.[22]

He criticized "Red-Headed Woman" because in it:

A girl is presented as physically irresistible, intent upon conquering her victims as they appear. As a stenographer she starts with her employer. After wrecking his home she proceeds spectacularly from one affair to another . . . [the film] is an exposition of the theory that the wages of sin are wealth, luxury and social position . . .[23]

Similarly, "Baby Face" was frowned upon by Quigley because it was the story of a beautiful woman and how:

As she passes from one lover to another she accumulates an increasing store of wealth, social position, and popularity. In the end, seemingly as a reward for a well-calculated life, she is married happily under prosperous circumstances.[24]

From our contemporary vantage point we might disparage some of Quigley's concerns, but his successful publishing of trade and fan magazines, along with an examination of the moral scruples then informing American popular culture, indicates that he was in touch with the opinions of millions of moviegoers. Hays and the industry's public relations committee kept promising that movies more to the liking of those millions would be produced, but movie industry performance did not change.[25]

Hays kept making excuses. By the 1930s he could blame the Depression for film content, proclaiming that "Many executives were desperate and many producers willing to take a chance." Once again seeing "mistakes" rather than deliberate intentions, Hays wrote that "It was inevitable that mistakes should have been made. Factors apparently beyond anyone's control played directly upon whatever human weakness there may have been."[26]

Hays appointment postponed large public protests by a decade; in that sense, the public relations campaign was very successful. There had always been protests: As early as 1924 some organizations withdrew from the public relations committee and called it a "smoke screen, an obvious camouflage, an approval stamp for the salacious films and for the questionable, if not criminal, conduct of the industry and its employees." But most Hollywood watchers stuck with Hays for a long time.[27]

Hays' presence also had worked political wonders. For instance, when Federal legislation to establish a licensing bureau known as the Federal Motion Picture Commission was picking up support, President Calvin Coolidge declared himself opposed and stated that the producers themselves were reforming the industry. Proof of this, he said, was the appointment of Will Hays, who "has been a most helpful influence in this work. . ." Federal censorship bills were repeatedly tabled, and the threatened onslaught of increased and toughened state censorship was put off.[28]

But during the early 1930s, industry critics showed increasing concern about film effects on international as well as domestic audiences. Hays himself argued that moviemakers:

> were important to their country, as trade no longer followed the flag, it now followed the films. If American pictures, shown everywhere, were to reflect credit on and not contempt of the American way of life, the ladies and gentlemen of Hollywood must henceforth regard themselves as ambassadors of Hollywood and of America.[29]

Hays was right on the statistics; over two-thirds of all movies shown in most European and Latin American countries during the 1930's were American films, and other countries also relied on the Hollywood product. But reports about the effects of American films abroad increasingly served as a depressant. For instance, *The Literary Digest* reported in 1934 that:

> China, Japan, Turkey, and several European countries have complained with increasing bitterness against some of Hollywood's portrayals of American life and have wondered whether Americans actually are given over to orgiastic enterprise.[30]

Also during the early 1930's, an Uruguay newspaper editor complained that American pictures concentrated on "cabaret life, the sins of society, and crime." American films in India, it was reported, were "proving a hindrance to amicable relations, because foreign audiences gain false and unfavorable impressions of the United States." The London *Daily Telegraph* observed that "people regard an American as a lawless, immoral individual, who carries a gun in his pocket at all times."[31] Another London newspaper stated that:

There is a flood of demoralizing screen stuff coming from the states . . . How America can permit these contemptible pictures of her youth and of her society to be distributed over the civilized world, passes understanding.[32]

The concerns seemed worldwide. A New Zealand movie theater owner complained in a movie trade magazine that in his country:

you could not persuade even a fifteen-year-old boy that there is an honest American businessman, politician, judge or jury . . . The American picture producer has taught us to believe that clean, honest courts of justice; clean, honest home life; clean, honest sport, are not known in the United States.[33]

One correspondent in Great Britain summed up the problem by stating that:

America's most powerful and pernicious spokesman in Europe today is Hollywood. The dominant type of motion picture which Hollywood is now exporting abroad is fuel, both to prejudice and to misunderstanding about the people and government of the United States. It is spreading, with very little opportunity to stop it, a false picture of America.[34]

As more reports of these kinds emerged, tensions over Hollywood's product grew. In 1929 one magazine argued that Hays and Jason Joy were men "whose occupation it is to shield, for enormous salaries, the panderers who have made their millions selling vice, crime and sexual suggestion . . . " In 1929 *The Literary Digest* observed of movies generally, "The last few years' standards are much lower. Mr. Hays' much boasted control has not helped any."[35]

The theme of broken promises became a prominent one in the growing criticism of Hays and Hollywood. A booklet of the International Reform Federation, "Broken Promises of the Motion Picture Industry," called Hays a liar. Similarly, the Federal Motion Picture Council of America, in its pamphlet "Responsibility for Better Motion Pictures," argued that:

The broken promises of the industry constitute a large section in the history of motion picture development . . . Promises have been broken so frequently that . . . federal legislation for the supervision and regulation of the production, distribution, advertising, and exhibition of films [is needed].[36]

Industry public relations was putting off the day of reckoning, but was apparently creating pressure to move from calls for community boycott to plans for governmental censorship.

By 1933 the National Committee of Parents and Teachers, in its magazine *Child Welfare*, was summarizing what it believed to be the lesson of years of frustration:

> We have tried cooperation with the motion picture industry for twenty-four years without success . . . The evidence before the public shows the utter futility of all cooperation with these agencies.[37]

The initial response of movie producers to this frustration domestic and foreign was merely "more of the same." In 1933 the MPPDA "added a renewal of dedication to our original objectives, as set forth back in 1922, 'to establish and maintain the highest possible moral and artistic standards of motion picture production.' " Producers were like those who know how easy it is to quit smoking after doing it many times: "The leaders again acknowledged their responsibility to the public for strict maintenance of the standards and purposes that had been adopted."[38]

But even Hays admitted that movie industry public relations-as-usual would no longer work in 1934, because public patience was exhausted: "There were unmistakable signs that a change had to come. Some American pictures were barred in nearly all foreign countries. Both the Studio Relations Committee and I were roundly upbraided by press and public."[39]

The negative feelings toward the movie industry finally received institutional backing in 1934 from the U.S. Bishops' Committee of the Catholic Church, which proposed that a "Legion of Decency" sign pledges not to go to those movies that attacked "traditional values." Even so, if only Catholics had been offended, the movie industry might have been able to tough it out.

That did not happen, because the campaign to "clean up the movies" proved to have great support in many different population groups. It was widely acknowledged that a majority of moviegoers supported the Legion's activities.[40] By April, 1934, millions of boycott pledges had been signed, and Hollywood leaders belatedly became alarmed. Hays later described the surge of pledge-signing as "an avenging fire, seeking to clean as it burned."[41]

The variety of groups that officially enlisted in or voiced support for the Legion is evident from the following partial list: the Chicago Church Foundation, the New York State Council of Churches, the Central Conference of Jewish Rabbis, the North Carolina Baptist Convention, the United Presbyterian Assembly, the Massachusetts Civil League, the National Conference of Jews and Christians, the Christian Endeavor Union, the Philadelphia Federation of Churches, the Hartford Federation of Churches, the Oregon Methodist Conference, the B'nai B'rith, the Moral and Social Welfare Committee of the Lutheran Church, the Jewish Welfare Board, the National Education Association, the Federal Council of Churches of Christ in America, the New

York Metropolitan League of Jewish Community Organizations, the Elks, the Masons, the Odd Fellows, the National Council of Jewish Women, the Episcopal Church's general convention, the International Council of Women . . . and the list could go on for pages and pages. These groups had not been always hostile to movie fare, but in 1934 they were fed up with "broken promises."[42]

The Legion of Decency campaign expanded through newspaper and magazine articles, discussions at lay and fraternal organizations, and mass meetings and marches. As one scholar who examined in detail the mechanism of the Legion campaign concluded,

> to an extraordinary degree the local campaigns preceded independently of each other. Each chose its own time to begin recruiting. . . . Each adopted its own technique. Some held mass-meetings and public demonstrations, while others adopted a quieter tone. Each had its own tempo. Some did all the recruiting on one day, while others proceeded at a more gradual pace.[43]

The campaign was extraordinarily effective. Because the movement was decentralized, it is hard to get accurate figures on the total number of pledge-signers, but reports from the time indicate that 10 or 11 million persons signed during the first ten weeks after the campaign began in April, 1934, and millions more afterwards.[44]

The campaign, although led by Catholics, was also ecumenical. One Catholic bishop wrote that, "Within the writer's own diocese Protestants of several cities have set Catholics an example by securing pledges from their people." A typical report came from the Savannah diocese: "The number of pledges amounted to several thousand in excess of the total Catholic population of Georgia, because of the request from nonCatholics for copies." The Protestant magazine *Christian Century* editorialized:

> It has been heartening to see the Protestant reaction to the launching of this Catholic crusade. Seldom has there been as clear an illustration of the essential unity of purpose of the religious bodies in the realm of social and moral action.[45]

Although the initial response from the movie studio heads was one of skepticism, trade and fan magazines reported that "Forty million customers are asking for purity" and *would* stay away from the theaters if film content did not change; because the average weekly attendance was about 70 million, that estimate, if true, was obviously threatening. The theater receipts show that the Legion packed a punch; in June, 1934, weekly national film attendance fell off by 15 million paid admissions.[46]

City by city, results came in; for instance, when Cardinal Dougherty of Philadelphia distributed a letter urging moviegoers "to register their united protest against immoral and indecent films by remaining away entirely from all motion picture theaters," theater audiences in that city declined by over 50 percent.[47]

Within a month, the manager of the Warner Brothers chain (which controlled much of Philadelphia movie exhibition) had to talk of closing all of his theaters, and movie company presidents convened a panicky meeting in New York:

> There was Harry Warner, standing up at the head of the table, shedding tears the size of horse turds, and pleading for someone to get him off the hook. And well he should, for you could fire a *cannon* down the center aisle of any theater in Philadelphia, without danger of hitting anyone! And there was Barney Balaban, watching him in terror, wondering if he was going to be next in Chicago, and Nick Schenck, wondering when he was going to be hit by a bucket of shit in New York.[48]

The producers truly had no idea about what to do. For a dozen years their public relations apparatus had forestalled such boycotts, and they thought that a few new pious statements and lists of "Do"s and "Don't"s would suffice once again. When the easy outs this time provided no exit, the producers had to do what they had long dreaded. They were forced to establish a self-censorship bureau with teeth and claws.

For instance, to placate the Legion of Decency, the MPPDA was forced to eliminate the Hollywood Jury and establish a well-staffed Production Code Administration (PCA) office. Producers would have to accept PCA recommendations unless they wanted to enter into a difficult New York appeals process from which few producers were to emerge victorious.[49]

Harder still was the provision that scripts had to be submitted to the PCA *before* the start of production. In addition, every MPPDA member was required to agree that he would not exhibit in his theaters any picture that did not bear the PCA seal of approval. Anyone who did not abide by these restrictions would have to pay a fine of $25,000.[50]

These were stiff requirements, but producers still probably would have found ways to get around them if it were not for the one other element insisted on by Legion of Decency leaders: the appointment of Joseph Breen as PCA head. Breen was in many ways the opposite of Hays; to put it simply, Breen did not trust others generally, and producers specifically.

Breen, after growing up in the rough Fairmount neighborhood of Philadelphia, had worked for 14 years on newspapers in Philadelphia, Washington and Chicago, then taken several short-term jobs before becoming Quigley's assistant for evaluating movie morality. He had the confidence of Legion of Decency leaders, who saw in him not only a graduate of Catholic schools and the Jesuit College of St. Joseph, but a person who forthrightly

told producers in 1934 that "pulpit, press and public were not in the usual gul-
lible mood to swallow the same old whitewash hokum which the industry had
so successfully employed in the past to smother anti-movie movements."[51]

As with Hays, though, the quick biography only brushes lightly the char-
acteristics of the man. Breen was not a Hays or a Jason Joy, but he was—as a
1935 profile in *Esquire* described him—a "hard-boiled, two-fisted Irishman
who can outshout the pick of Hollywood hog-callers."[52] He made life miserable for directors and produceres who wanted some flexibility and hated the
tough enforcement of the Code on which the Legion and Breen insisted.
Breen, who remained head of the Production Code Administration for 20
years after 1934, was the czar in reality that Hays was only by popular
phrase-making.

For instance, when Breen tried to convince the redoubtable Harry Cohn
of Columbia Studios that he meant business, Cohn looked through Breen's
papers and said, "What's all this shit?" Breen replied, "Mr. Cohn—I take that
as a compliment." When the startled Cohn asked what he meant, Breen said,
"My friends inform me that if there's any expert in this town on shit—it's you.
So if I have to be judged, I'm glad it's by professionals."[53] When another producer complained that Breen was turning the movie industry into such a
bland operation that it would be better for producers to go into the milk business, Breen kicked him out of his office, vowing that he would "free the
screen" of "whorehouse crap."[54]

To Hollywood producers and directors, Breen was a villain on whom neither honey nor vinegar had an effect.[55] According to film historian Robert
Sklar, Breen and the code hindered development of mature cinema themes.[56]
Whatever the effect, the history of movie public relations from 1921 through
1934 shows that producers brought tough code enforcement on themselves.

There was ample opportunity year after year, until the Legion struck, to
develop a peace treaty with moderate community groups, but Hollywood
leaders preferred attempts at public relations deception. They promised and
promised and hired Hays to be chief promiser. Their strategy was successful
for a while, but if a sucker is born every minute, suckers who have been fooled
too often may become born-again crusaders. Then, the deal that eventually is
struck may be worse for both sides, and worse for a public that likes entertainment within flexible bounds.

CHAPTER SEVEN

Come the Depression:
Corporate Public Relations and
the National Recovery Administration

The discussion of the movie industry in chapter six illustrated the outcome of one half of the Ivy Lee prescription: Get a czar. The other half stressed that companies should lobby to avoid competition whenever possible. This chapter describes the progress in that direction of corporate pilgrims during the first half of the 1930s.

Following the stock market crash, many business leaders blamed competition for economic problems. For instance, trade association management-consultant Charles W. Stevenson wrote that money-losing large companies were being "crucified on the cross of competition." Stevenson's proposal, a typical one for this period, was that each industry establish government-enforced prices and production quotas, with new entrants allowed in only after approval by established companies.[1]

Stevenson wanted voluntary change, but other business spokesmen, such as General Electric president Gerard Swope, wanted government-backed power to force the issue. At a September, 1931, meeting of the National Electrical Manufacturers Association, Swope called for "mandatory government of industry" by trade associations dominated by large companies and backed up by state power.[2] Swope and his public relations associate, J. G. Frederick, produced a book designed to show that, "One cannot loudly call for more stability in business and get it on a purely voluntary basis."[3]

Legalized cartels were not popular with the public, though. Silas Strawn, spokesman for the Chamber of Commerce, and James Emery, counsel for the National Association of Manufacturers, both argued during the early 1930s that an attempt to impose cartels would bring enormous opposition.[4] Robert

Lamont, leaving the Hoover Administration to be spokesman for the American Iron and Steel Institute, said in 1930 that cartel-legalizing proposals "can never pass Congress in the present state of public opinion."[5]

Public opinion, however, became volatile as the Depression unravelled some traditional economic beliefs. Any plan projected to increase employment could win favor. Chamber of Commerce Chairman Julius Barnes told automobile executive Roy Chapin, in April, 1931, that the public would now support moves to "eliminate much destructive competition," as long as they were coupled with programs to increase employment.[6] Similarly, Swope suggested a public relations strategy based on a pledge to "tie" expanded employment to "a modification [of antitrust laws] which would give us more latitude. . ."[7]

Such suggestions received considerable corporate applause from publications such as *Business Week*, association leaders such as National Association of Manufacturers President James Edgerton, and corporate executives in many fields. If the public could be brought along, it would then be possible to pressure all businesses to join in, as Swope's colleague Owen Young argued: "Cooperation is required by the great majority of the participants and the coercion of the rest may ultimately be necessary."[8]

Ironically enough, a major big-business stumbling block in 1931 and 1932 was President Herbert Hoover, generally lambasted for being too cozy with corporations. Hoover did not believe that giving corporate executives governmental authority would lead to more jobs. He decided to fight plans such as those of Swope, publicly complaining in September, 1931, that the Swope Plan's price-fixing would:

> bring into existence such a union of forces in the industrial world as has never been dreamed of before. It would lead to the creation of a series of monopolies . . . and the public would be called upon to bear the burden.[9]

Hoover himself claimed that he lost big business' support by not buckling; clearly, Franklin Roosevelt in 1932 did pick up some significant corporate support. For instance, astute public relations executives such as new Chamber of Commerce president H. I. Harriman and Robert Lund of the National Association of Manufacturers both exuded sympathy; Harriman was "antiHoover" and "very friendly to the whole Roosevelt campaign," and Lund called the 1932 Democratic platform "our Party Platform." While historians still debate the full extent of corporate support for Roosevelt, it is clear that in 1933 big business had excellent ties to the Roosevelt administration, and was justified in expecting a piece of the policy action.[10]

Those markers were called in during the spring of 1933, as corporate leaders pushed for a government–business partnership bill that became known as the National Industrial Recovery Act. Chamber president Harriman, National Industrial Conference Board President Virgil Jordan, trade-association attorneys David Podell and Gilbert Montague, corporate executives Swope, Malcolm Rorty, James Rand, and others, were able to work well with liberal supporters of national economic planning such as Rexford Tugwell, Jerome Frank, and Robert Wagner.[11]

The partnership idea of corporatists and leftists, keystone of the original New Deal conception, received great support from Washington corporate representatives. Secretary of Labor Frances Perkins remarked that at Congressional hearings the businessmen were the radicals. "Compared to them," she said, "I'm a conservative. They're willing to go to any length of government regulation if it will get them out of their troubles . . . "[12] Business Week reported that Chamber of Commerce leaders "are ready to subscribe to the idea of governmental control of business to a degree that would have seemed incredible a year ago."[13]

Harriman was perhaps the most influential cheerleader. He continued his election support of Roosevelt throughout 1933 and even told a Congressional committee that he would favor a Constitutional amendment giving the President power to control industry. Harriman's pitch was a standard Progressive stress on the inevitability of what appeared to be progress: The "laissez-faire economy, which worked admirably in earlier and simpler industrial life must be replaced by a philosophy of planned national economy."[14]

Other corporate representatives were applauders. When Franklin Roosevelt spoke to the national meeting of the U.S. Chamber of Commerce in May, 1933, he was greeted with "an enthusiasm which can hardly be overemphasized." At that meeting Harriman offered him instant placement in the American pantheon, telling Chamber members that "Never in the history of the nation has an Administration more courageously and fairly attempted to deal with so many and such far-reaching problems." Harriman had broad support: 27 of 49 speakers at the Chamber meeting also called for more government direction of industry.[15]

So did others from the corporate realm. The National Association of Manufacturers supported the NRA. Goodyear Tire and Rubber Co. spokesman P. W. Litchfield proposed "substantial concessions to what we have in the past classified as the more radical school of thought."[16]

Link-Belt Co. spokesman George Torrance suggested appointment of an "industry dictator" for each major industry. The dictator would be authorized to set production schedules, prices, wage rates, and just about everything else. One executive proposed that companies wanting to compete in the traditional ways should be denied use of the U.S. mail.[17]

The corporate public relations message was summarized in Business Week's May, 1933, suggestion that:

> The American business man at this moment is utterly weary of the ruthless
> competitive struggle . . . He is willing, he feels just now, to surrender some part
> of his freedom of action to achieve a degree of stability.[18]

The result of the corporate push was a bill that would allow some smaller competitors to rest, sometimes for good. Under the legislation hammered out,
large corporations would be allowed to have the trade associations that they
often controlled establish codes binding on their smaller competitors.

This National Industrial Recovery Act (NIRA) went far beyond reasonable revocation of some antitrust provisions. Instead, it allowed legally enforceable establishment of favorable prices for some products and unfavorable ones for others, with the result that companies powerful enough to write
the rules could help themselves and hurt others.[19]

Industry by industry, major companies won. The Steel Code, for instance,
was largely controlled by United States Steel and Bethlehem, because those
two companies alone had over half the voting strength of their "code authority." As historian Broadus Mitchell noted:

> In general the members of a code authority were chosen by a minority of firms in
> an industry, often by a small minority of the most powerful . . . smaller and scat
> tered business units were underrepresented on code authorities, labor and con
> sumers were practically not represented at all.[20]

Overall, over 700 codes were established under NIRA, with implementation made possible by about 11,000 Federal administrative orders and 70 Presidential executive orders. Almost every business transaction came under an
NIRA classification, from Automobile Manufacturing and Cotton Textiles
to Lightning Rod Manufacturing and Corn Cob Pipes.

Groups that were competitively successful faced the prospect of losing
their advantages because of political coercion. Four hundred codes allowed
for the fixing of minimum prices so that major companies could not be
undersold. Other provisions in many codes restricted trade-in allowances,
credit terms, competition in quality, or reduction of prices based on geographical proximity. Thirty industries even received governmental backing
to limit the construction of new plants or prevent the opening of closed ones,
even though such provisions obviously cut against the announced purpose of
job creation.[21]

The check on possible abuses was supposed to be the National Recovery
Administration itself, in its role as expediter and reviewer of industry codes,
and enforcer when necessary. But NRA administrator Hugh Johnson and his
key assistants – Alvin Brown, Robert Lea, Kenneth Simpson, Arthur D.
Whiteside, Clarence Williams, and others – not only had large corporate
backgrounds (often a vital preparation for their work) but also shared a prefer

ence for greater economic concentration and a dislike for entrepreneurial competition. The result, according to one observer, was that complaints tended to end up in a "bargain between business leaders on one hand and businessmen in the guise of government officials on the other."[22]

Such a view is born out by close analysis of the codes as a whole. As historian Ellis Hawley concluded,

> Most of the price clauses were directed against price cutting by "little fellows." In numerous industries . . . small firms often existed only because they offered lower prices to offset consumer preferences for advertised brands, prices sometimes made possible by lower wage rates, sometimes by more favorable location, sometimes by other advantages arising out of specialization or recapitalization. It was in the interest of larger firms, therefore, to eliminate price and wage differentials and wipe out the special advantages that made them possible. In general, the majority of the codes did move in this direction.[23]

Those who would send corporate representatives to Washington found that knowing how to get around the capital was beginning to pay more than production or marketing adeptness. According to one observer, on the road to Washington, were:

> groups of excited businessmen from the same line of industry working until late at night putting the finishing touches on what they wanted Washington to sanction—because once these codes were approved and had been signed by the President their provisions were legally enforceable . . . [Washington was filled with] codifiers, coordinators and all the great assemblage of other seekers after light and lucre.[24]

Governmental expansion in 1933 was largely a corporate enterprise. NRA Administrator Hugh Johnson noted correctly that it was corporate leaders, not governmental New Dealers, who insisted on government-imposed reductions of business freedom: "There was not one single code that industry did not propose and beg to have applied." Conservative columnist Frank Kent wrote of the "enthusiasm of the industrialists," with their visions of "competition eliminated, prices raised, profits assured and every business man put on Easy Street."[25]

Leaders of industry who made up the National Civic Federation early in the 20th century, along with prophetic public relations counselors such as Ivy Lee, had long been working toward intra-industry "cooperation." Now, the dream was becoming a reality. Industry by industry, stories of anticompetitive moves stand out.

In the tire industry, for instance, Harvey Firestone did not like being undersold by "special-brand distributors" who featured cut-rate prices and large trade-in allowances on used tires. Such distributors, according to Firestone, put pressure on tire manufacturers "to meet the prices of the special-brand tires or be eliminated from the business."[26]

Firestone did not want to meet prices, so he used political means to try to eliminate the special-brand dealers from the business. He and his colleagues from other major companies developed and had the NRA accept a Retail Rubber Tire and Battery Trade Code, which called such price cutting an unfair method of competition. Firestone was one of the leading cheerleaders for NRA and was quick to send FDR telegrams promising "to adopt and to put your program into effect." The world would be made safe for more costly tires.[27]

Such examples pose an obvious question: How would the public be made to sit still for conduct that ran against traditional economic beliefs? Would the public applaud as the economic interests of those businesses without political clout lost out? How could government-corporate collaborationism be sold?

Part of the public sales resistance, of course, had been eliminated by the Depression; some individuals were willing to try almost anything for a while. Still, Americans basically believed that competition was healthy. Leaders knew that extraordinary public relations efforts would be required to shake that belief. "Public opinion must be marshalled," Bernard Baruch insisted in a Brookings Institution speech on "Economic Planning and Government Control." *Business Week* noted that "the President has the power" to become an economic dictator, but his goal was to "rely at first largely on the vast power of public opinion."[28]

The first step in gaining public backing involved the display of carrots that Swope and others had suggested: Promises of jobs and recovery. James Rand, a member of the NRA Steering Committee, announced in May, 1933, that his Committee for the Nation, working together with the National Association of Manufacturers, had a plan to put 3 million men back to work—if an NRA was established. The Chamber of Commerce's Harriman told the House Labor Committee in late April that trade-association control of individual businesses would lead to recovery within 30 days. Overall, corporate executives were "lavishly promising a dramatic improvement in the unemployment rate if the antitrust barriers were let down."[29]

The second step relied on corporate sticks: Large companies were asked to make sure that their employees showed NRA enthusiasm. At IBM, for instance, company publications promoted the NRA, company employees were ordered to march in NRA parades, and company executives regularly made favorable comments about public–private partnership. Company spokesmen anticipated Orwell in their attempts to turn white into black: In hundreds of corporate speeches, free competition became known as "cannibalism," classical economists became "old dealers," reduced-price sales became "cut-throat price slashing," and those who produced bargains became "chiselers."[30]

The NRA soon demanded that all of its advocates use the new vocabulary. Companies joined with the Administration in distributing handbooks with titles such as *Pointed Paragraphs for Speakers.* Economic collusion was renamed "cooperation," elimination of competition became "codes of fair competition," and "ethical behavior" was defined as forced maintenance of prices. The new style of thought at times seemed pervasive; for instance, at one business convention a skeptical reporter noted much "talk about freedom . . . freedom from too much free enterprise, too much individual initiative, and much too much competition."[31]

The general pressure to join in was backed throughout the second half of 1933 by a publicized flow of executive speeches and interviews. One day Alfred I. du Pont would suggest that corporations should be "free from inordinate competition." Then a leading shipbuilder, C. L. Bardo, would call the NRA-creating bill "the most important legislation ever enacted." P. S. du Pont, Alfred Sloan, and others who later broke with the New Deal, joined Swope and other "progressive businessmen" in making kind comments about the NRA during 1933.[32]

When some started doubting, H. F. Sinclair, chairman of Consolidated Oil, could be quoted to the effect that governmental regulation "all the way from the derrick to the service station" would be the industry's best friend. Frank Phillips, president of Phillips Petroleum, would then chime in, "The NRA is going to succeed and we are going to succeed."[33]

For those still unswayed by promises of bread, circuses were provided. NRA public relations practitioners in Washington worked with corporate staffs to develop symbols, songs, mass spectaculars, and other publicity devices.

Most famous of the symbols was the Blue Eagle, which every company was pressured to display. Hugh Johnson explained the Blue Eagle's function: "To play any game, you must of course know who you are playing with and who against. That is the reason for baseball uniforms and that is the reason for the Blue Eagle." Those displaying the Blue Eagle were virtuous, Johnson suggested, and those without it were enemies of the people: "All we want is to make very clear just what side everybody is playing on."[34]

Blue Eagles appeared on placards, gummed labels, and flags; on store windows, office doors, and newspaper pages; in the patterns of ties, dresses, and even tattoos. Blue Eagle banners were rushed to NRA offices across the country and distributed to businesses. Public relations managers organized hundreds of thousands of schoolchildren to go door to door asking for pledges to buy products only from Blue Eagle businesses. NRA speakers' bureaus even included Hugh Johnson's 77-year-old mother. She warned citizens at a Tulsa rally that, "People had better obey the NRA because my son will enforce it like lightning, and you can never tell where lightning will strike."[35]

NRA songs were also useful in developing public support. They had lyrics such as:

> Join the good old NRA, Boys, and we will end this awful strife.
> Join it with the spirit that will give the Eagle life . . .
> How the Nation shouted when they heard the joyful news!
> We're going back to work again, and that means bread and shoes.

New oaths of allegiance were designed. On Boston Common, Mayor James Curley (out of jail for a time) and 100,000 schoolchildren said in unison:

> I promise as a good American citizen to do my part for the NRA. I will buy only where the Blue Eagle flies . . . I will help President Roosevelt bring back good times.[36]

Corporations gave employees release time to march in mass NRA parades; some individuals, moved by the fervor and hoping for economic recovery, joined in voluntarily. Two hundred bands and 250,000 individuals marched down New York's Fifth Avenue on September 13, 1933, and saluted an NRA flag 90 feet long and 75 feet wide: "The eyes of the Blue Eagle measured a foot across." Business and government public relations practitioners set up smaller parades in other cities.

Skillful orchestration of press releases highlighted the supposed success of the public–private partnership throughout the country. Press release subjects included proclamations of supposed recovery in Kansas City; town meetings of praise for the NRA throughout Texas; and one quarter of the population of Springfield, Missouri, participating in a march. Some stories were exaggerated, others accurately reflected the combination of public despair and whipped-up popular furor; all seemed to receive first-class publicist handling.[38]

Johnson understood the uses of public relations. A former businessman, he had been one of Roosevelt's speechwriters and issue analysts before his promotion, and he believed that words made deeds. Johnson loved to use religious metaphors, especially when speaking about the "Holy Thing" which was the NRA, "the Greatest Social Advance Since the Days of Jesus Christ." He compared his critics to "Judases" and responded to complaints by writing, "I often think of Moses. His NRA was a code of only ten short articles and according to latest reports it isn't working perfectly even yet—after some 4,000 years of trial and error and even after the great reorganization of the years 30 to 34 A.D."[39]

Johnson, with corporate associates, tried hard through public relations to convince individuals to ignore economic rationality and spend whatever they had saved. "People who have a little left have adopted a nonbuying policy," he complained in one speech. "We must shake ourselves out of this 4-year-old idea of doing without against a rainy day and we must do that overnight . . . Buy! Buy now! . . ."[40]

Johnson also had enormous faith in the power of public-opinion pressure. He said that anyone who broke with NRA code restrictions by lowering prices in his shop would be in trouble:

> The NRA will break the bright sword of his commercial honor in the eyes of his neighbors – and throw the fragments – in scorn – in the dust at his feet. It is a sentence of economic death. It will never happen. The threat of it transcends any puny penal provision in this law.[41]

By 1934, though, it was apparent that the NRA was not working. A study by the liberal Brookings Institution found that the economy was not recovering: One and one-half million jobs had been added during the first year of NRA, but only through work spreading, not job creation. Brookings scholars noted that both hourly wages and living costs had increased by about 9 to 10% during that year, so the average loss in real wages was 5 to 6%. Brookings concluded that "the NRA, on the whole, retarded recovery."[42]

Under pressure from Senator William Borah, the NRA was forced to hold hearings in January, 1934, concerning complaints about the NRA from small businessmen. Borah said his office had received over 9 thousand complaints. Johnson wanted the hearings to be a carefully-controlled vindication of NRA policies, so the NRA "Consumers' Advisory Board" he had agreed to establish was at first kept from presenting its critical findings. The press found "gagging" of the board a conflict story too good to pass up, and the NRA had its first thoroughly unfavorable publicity.[43]

The pressure accelerated as Borah, a wonderful orator, began giving a series of public and Senate chamber speeches. In February, 1934, he gave a radio talk about price-fixing by large corporations and destruction of small businesses, noting that:

> When these conditions are pointed out, someone goes into a trance and begins to ejaculate about how we cannot go back to rugged individualism; that we have arrived at a new era, the era of planned industrialism.

Whatever the public relations label, Borah said such railroading was a "travesty upon justice."[44]

Following his speech, Borah received more than 18,000 requests for help from small businessmen and publicized many of them. NRA public relations practitioners had planned out their general lines of publicity, but they were not able to anticipate a single senator refusing to play ball, nor a newspaper columnist such as Frank Kent of the *Baltimore Sun* constantly hounding them.

A great rift between large corporations and small businessmen developed. Small businesses pushed for elimination of price and production controls and restoration of free markets, but Kent continued to point out "the great love of the Big Business Man for the NRA." Companies such as Bethlehem Steel had written into codes strategically advantageous policies, and Eugene Grace, Bethlehem's head, was still speaking "with glowing approval of what the NRA has done for industry." The NRA system itself, though, began breaking down in late 1934.[45]

Many NRA codes were proving to be unmanageable. Typically, the lumber industry's price schedules and production quota systems were so complicated that regulators could not understand them well enough to enforce them. Disputes broke out in other industries as well. Even worse, from a public relations standpoint, were those situations in which enforcement had been vigilant. Kent and others began writing human-interest stories about individuals such as the pants-presser undergoing prosecution because he had pressed a pair of pants for 39 cents instead of 75 cents. Publicity such as this the NRA did not need.[46]

By 1935, small businesses were beginning to openly defy the NRA codes. In the service trades, code price-fixing provisions were especially hard to enforce because consumers favored those who offered bargains. Mail-order houses and small manufacturers openly defied the plumbing fixtures code. Minimum price schedules had to be revised or removed in the mop, shoe polish and twine industries. Senator Borah told his constituents to disregard NRA codes, fees, and fines, and tell him of any enforcement attempts. Hugh Johnson could no longer count on his dream of overwhelming public support making legal enforcement unnecessary; Johnson himself was relieved of his position and told to take an extended vacation.[47]

In June, 1935, with Congress scheduled to decide whether to renew the NRA, corporate public-relations practitioners tried to get the bandwagon rolling again. Corporate-sponsored rallies in New York and Washington attracted 1,700 and 1,500 businessmen, respectively. Practitioners from the retailing, textiles, coal, steel, paper, drug, tobacco, and copper industries all spoke for NRA extension; their repeated explanation was that we must adopt to "present day needs and not the economic society of 50 years ago."[48]

Proto-Orwellian language once again dominated NRA discourse. For instance, textile industry spokesman G. H. Dorr, when asked whether NRA codes collided with individual rights, said:

What is this boasted freedom that we talk about? . . . It is ordinarily only through the collective action of a code that the majority can get the 'liberty' to conduct their business by the competitive methods and standards that they desire.[49]

The Supreme Court temporarily settled the matter. In May, 1935, the Court unanimously declared the NRA to be unconstitutional. If the Constitution's commerce clause were interpreted as broadly as the Administration wanted, the Court argued, "federal authority would embrace practically all the activities of the people," and that was not what the framers of the Constitution had in mind.[50]

Following the Supreme Court decision, Kent noted that the "tremendous manufactured NRA enthusiasm" was all gone. The hype followed by reality "does leave the American people looking foolish," he commented. "Never has a nation been put in a more ridiculous position. We are right back where we started."[51]

Not quite. There was still the matter of the public commitment made by corporate leaders: If given their way, they had promised, increased employment and prosperity would result. This public contract had not been fulfilled, and the result was greater public animosity toward big business. Significantly, the stock market crash by itself did not turn the public generally against large corporations, nor did the reports of misconduct revealed in 1932 by Senate Banking and Currency Committee hearings. Most members of the public were uninvolved in such matters, and they still trusted traditional societal leaders to make things right.

The public did become heavily involved in the NRA, however. The involvement was by necessity, if the plan was to work; for Johnson and others saw courts of public opinion, rather than courts of justice, essential to NRA enforcement. Marches, songs, and Blue Eagle placards succeeded in focusing public attention on the NRA. The success enventually backfired. When corporate leaders were perceived as having fallen down on their side of the bargain—production of new jobs and economic recovery—the public turned on them. By the late 1930s the Chamber of Commerce accurately could note that business had become "the country's Number One whipping boy." It took a long time for the pain of that whipping to go away. Perhaps it hurt even more because the whipping was warranted.

CHAPTER EIGHT

Bringing "Order Out of Chaos": The Public Relations Theory of Edward Bernays

Let's review for a moment: In many public statements by leading business-men during the 1920s and 1930s, an arrogant frankness was apparent. Before the Depression, for instance, A. B. Farquhar of the National Association of Manufacturers contended that:

> The manufacturer is a great constructor. He gives the country its wealth. It comes from him. The manufacturer is by far the most important of all classes. No class could do without him. We would be living in caves, dressed in skins to-day, except for him.[1]

Publicist Charles Fay wrote that Americans should and would obey business executives, for "Most of us instinctively recognize big men, and cheerfully take the orders of our betters. . ."[2]

Even during the early years of the Depression many public relations practi-tioners were advocating not just stiff upper lips but continued expressions of superiority as well. One writer in *Nation's Business* contended that "the busi-nessman of today" is "mature, cultivated, sure of himself in every relation of life, accepting leadership as by natural right, a man never stooping to bluster or brag because he never feels the need of it." Another *Nation's Business* writer argued that the American people and government must admit that business-men have "been given a peculiar ability to direct the energies of other men in the economic field."[3]

The public was hooting. Movie industry, NRA, and many other public re-lations failures showed that something more than a "trust me" approach was needed. In 1934 the *Saturday Evening Post* listed words routinely used to attack business executives: "Tory, reactionary, cannibal, obscene, adherent to the law of tooth and claw."[4]

For public relations as a business, however, bad news is good news. The railroad industry plunged into public relations when the public was no longer voluntarily greeting new track with enthusiasm. Utilities embraced public relations when they were criticized as swollen monopolies. As long as industry executives generally believed that the public *naturally* would accept their leadership, there would be little willingness to develop massive public relations budgets and staffs. But with Depression discrediting to be overcome, corporations were open to the approach of Edward Bernays, a person who distilled the experiences of railroad and utilities, movie magnates, NRA planners, and Ivy Lee, and then added his own beliefs in order to create the full rationale for modern public relations.

Bernays, nephew of Sigmund Freud, taught Depression-harrangued executives that "propaganda" (Bernays' word, used positively as the title of his major theoretical work) would make Americans respect them again.[5] He urged business leaders to speak of themselves as public servants and hide any big sticks they might possess. He wrote that intelligent individuals would defend public relations "propaganda" as "the modern instrument by which they can fight for productive ends and help to bring order out of chaos."[6]

Bernays is known to some historians for naming the field that he would influence so heavily. In 1922, while Ivy Lee was still referring to himself as a publicity advisor, publicity expert, or publicity director, Bernays was describing himself as a public-relations counsel, and that is the title that caught on.[7] But Bernays did something more important: He gave public relations practitioners pride in their activities.

He was able to do so because of his communication skills and a personal belief-structure made up of atheism, Freudianism, and a faith that behind-the-scenes controllers should exercise "social responsibility" by devising clever public-relations campaigns to direct "human herds" into appropriate corrals. After reading Bernays' writings from the 1920s and 1930s, I interviewed him in August, 1984, when he was 92 years old.[8] Remarkably, his presuppositions remained consistent throughout the decades.

Bernays' fundamental faith has been his lack of belief in God. He made this choice as a young adult and stuck with it, he said during our interview, pointing to a passage about himself and his sisters in his 1965 autobiography:

> None of us attended religious services or received religious instruction, nor did my father or mother discuss religion with us. Father believed that choice of religion was an individual's inherent right, to be exercised, if he wished, when he became an adult at eighteen or twenty-one. This is what he told his children.[9]

Bernays' choice was to believe in himself and his ability to "manipulate public opinion," as he put in forthrightly in the the title of an article published in the *American Journal of Sociology* in 1928.[10]

Some of Bernays' predecessors trusted in an "invisible hand" that controlled not only marketplaces but journalistic activities; truth would emerge from the clash of opinions not by chance, but because truth corresponded to the nature of God who had created the world and sustained it. Bernays, however, saw what he called in our interview "a world without God" rapidly descending into social chaos. Therefore, he contended that social manipulation by public relations counselors was justified by the end of creating man-made gods who could assert subtle social control and prevent disaster.[11]

The importance of atheism to Bernays' public relations concept is evident in interviews such as the one recorded in a 1932 *Atlantic Monthly* article. Bernays argued that, in the absence of public relations, society would be controlled by "the fortuitous and whimsical forces of life and chance." He said:

> There is something appalling to the ordinary business man in the fact that his business lies at the mercy of uncontrollable forces of whim and chance. . . . How can you blame the intelligent business man who has millions invested in his industry, and thousands dependent on it for jobs, if he attempts by intelligent propaganda to give these shifting tides of taste a direction which he can follow without loss; to control by means of propaganda what otherwise would be controlled disastrously by chance?[12]

In Bernays' world governed by chance, manipulation to prevent accident is true benevolence, thinly disguised. The rare magazine writer who caught this aspect of Bernays' belief generally was sarcastic. Stuart Chase wrote, "Not only God but Counsels of Public Relations are masters of the mystic pulls of gravitation."[13] But Bernays, seeing public relations counselors as masters in an otherwise masterless civilization, has always seen opinion "manipulators"–Bernays' word, used positively–as public servants. He said during our interview:

> We cannot have chaos. We have no being in the air to watch over us. We must watch over ourselves, and that is where public relations counselors can prove their effectiveness, by making the public believe that human gods are watching over us for our own benefit. . . . My uncle expressed this very well: People need sacred dances. Public relations counsels should be trained to call the tunes.[14]

The second breakthrough factor for Bernays was his faith in Freudianism, which came naturally because he was Sigmund Freud's nephew. (During our interview, as in the paragraph above, Bernays referred to Freud simply as, "My uncle."[15])

Sigmund Freud's personal charm obviously affected Bernays, judging from his written remembrance of when:

> Freud and I took long walks together through the woods that surrounded Carlsbad, he in pepper-and-salt knickerbockers, green Tyrolean hat with feather and ram's horn stuck in the hat band, brown hand-knit socks, heavy brown brogues and sturdy walking stick – and I in my Brooks Brothers suit. We walked quickly over the sloping hills, talking all the way. I wish I had taken notes and preserved what was said . . . [16]

Seventy years later, Bernays still spoke of those brief talks as a highlight of his life. He always wrote reverently of his uncle's doctrines, and he arranged for translation into English and publication in the United States of Freud's *General Introductory Lectures*. As Bernays wrote proudly, that publication was "the first popular presentation of psychoanalysis by Freud himself; it stimulated broad, widespread interest in psychoanalysis in this country."[17]

Bernays saw useful publicity aspects in the avuncular connection, and his harping on it became obnoxious at times. In 1960 when Bernays criticized a play about Freud, a headline in the show-business magazine *Variety* nastily referred to Bernays as a "professional nephew."[18] In many ways, though, it was the ideological component – not just Freud, but Freudianism – that was crucial for Bernays. Bernays stressed Freud's teaching that, in Bernays' words:

> many of man's thoughts and actions are compensatory substitutes for desires which he had been obliged to suppress. A thing may be desired not for its intrinsic worth or usefulness, but because he has unconsciously come to see in it a symbol of something else, the desire for which he is ashamed to admit to himself.[19]

Bernays then made the practical application: "The successful propagandist must understand the true motives and not be content to accept the reasons which men give for what they do."[20] The job of the public relations person, Bernays suggested, is to know his subjects better than they know themselves. That may not be hard, because men and women hardly know themselves at all:

> Universal literacy was supposed to educate the common man to control his environment. Once he could read and write he would have a mind fit to rule. So ran the democratic doctrine. But instead of a mind, universal literacy has given him rubber stamps, rubber stamps inked with advertising slogans, with editorials, with published scientific data, with the trivialities of the tabloids and the

platitudes of history, but quite innocent of original thought. Each man's rubber stamps are the duplicates of millions of others, so that when those millions are exposed to the same stimuli, all receive identical imprints.[21]

Bernays' view of the masses has been consistent over the years. In our interview Bernays still spoke of the primacy of mass emotion, even psychosis, over reason – "We live in an age of the id" – and said that if he were President of the United States he would:

> apply social psychology . . . by finding out what the learned men of our society project into the future and then developing a program to make sure that individuals are influenced by the best socially progressive views. I would develop themes of mutual adaptation and faith in governmental and corporate leadership that could then be implanted through public relations skills in the public generally . . . I would not leave our future in the hands of people who only function through their reactions.[22]

With such a threat from those directed by emotion rather than reason, Bernays has said that public relations counselors *must not* abide by the ordinary demands of ethics that might apply to them as individuals, but they *must* subordinate individual conscience to the need to save civilization from chaos. Pulling strings behind the scenes was necessary not for personal advantage but for social salvation.[23]

This third part of Bernays' trinity – not just atheism, not just Freudianism, but a rationale for public relations manipulation based on his lack of confidence in either God or man – was his most significant contribution to 20th-century public relations. Bernays not only sidestepped traditional ethical restraints, but substituted for them a positive command: Manipulate "so as to bring order out of chaos." As Bernays said during our interview, if it is useful to "shape information" into a fiction designed to preserve social stability, a public relations "professional," by Bernays' standards, is "obligated" to do so.[24]

Walter Lippmann had merely hinted at the shape of things to come in his book *Public Opinion* (1922), when he noted that:

> The development of the publicity man is a clear sign that the facts of modern life do not spontaneously take a shape in which they can be known. They must be given a shape by somebody, and since in the daily routine reporters cannot give a shape to facts, and since there is little disinterested organization of intelligence, the need for some formulation is being met by the interested parties.[25]

Bernays went further, first in *Crystallizing Public Opinion* (1923), which explained why "the groups and herd are the basic mechanism of public change,"[26] and particularly in his blunt book of 1928, *Propaganda*; its doctrines started to gain influence during the late 1930s.

Bernays began *Propaganda* with the assertion that:

> The conscious and intelligent manipulation of the organized habits and opinions of the masses is an important element in democratic society. Those who manipulate this unseen mechanism of society constitute an invisible government which is the true ruling power of our country.[27]

That was an awesome opening note. Because a democratic society is considered to be one in which "the people" in general do rule, and an authoritarian society is often considered one in which a small group of people rule, Bernays was trying to square the circle by arguing, in effect, that we must kill democracy to save it.

Others during the 1920s and 1930s had argued similarly, but they were not audacious enough to consider such a degree of social control "democratic." Bernays considered behind-the-scenes manipulation to be the type of "democracy" that was still practical:

> We are governed, our minds are molded, our tastes formed, our ideas suggested, largely by men we have never heard of. This is a logical result of the way in which our democratic society is organized. Vast numbers of human beings must cooperate in this manner if they are to live together as a smoothly functioning society.[28]

Bernays did not stop there, but contended repeatedly that such a behind-the-scenes system is the *only* one possible in a large-scale society seeking to avoid outright authoritarianism:

> Whatever attitude one chooses to take toward this condition, it remains a fact that in almost every act of our daily lives, whether in the sphere of politics or business, in our social conduct or our ethical thinking, we are dominated by the relatively small number of persons—a trifling fraction of our hundred and twenty million—who understand the mental processes and social patterns of the masses. It is they who pull the wires which control the public mind, who harness old social forces and govern us as to the orderly functioning of our group life.[29]

Without belief in the "invisible hand," Bernays saw behind-the-scenes wire-pullers as the only individuals standing between order and social chaos.

Bernays did not hesitate to argue, following Lippmann's example, that an authoritarian system of control (by wise, Platonic guardians, of course) could be preferable to the degradation of democracy that appeared essential:

It might be better to have, instead of propaganda and special pleading, committees of wise men who would choose our rulers, dictate our conduct, private and
public, and decide upon the best types of clothes for us to wear and the best
kinds of food for us to eat.[30]

But this was not going to happen:

We have chosen the opposite method, that of open competition. We must find a
way to make free competition function with reasonable smoothness. To achieve
this society has consented to permit free competition to be organized by leadership and propaganda.[31]

Once again, some would have hesitated to use the words "free competition"
alongside activities that might appear to favor the opposite of freedom, but
Bernays rushed in.

Bernays was not sanguine about all of the trends he described. He wrote
that, "The instruments by which public opinion is organized and focused may
be misused." He noted:

Some of the phenomena of this process are criticized—the manipulation of
news, the inflation of personality, and the general ballyhoo by which politicians
and commercial products and social ideas are brought to the consciousness and
the masses.[32]

But there was no alternative: "Such organization and focusing are necessary
to orderly life." For Bernays, there was no choice; there was no exit.[33]

Bernays not only went beyond his predecessors in developing the rationale
for a public relations style that prized manipulation; he also argued for a new
methodology. A sound practitioner, Bernays wrote:

takes account not merely of the individual, nor even of the mass mind alone but
also and especially of the anatomy of society, with its interlocking group forma-
tions and loyalties. [The individual is] a cell organized into the social unit.
Touch a nerve at a sensitive spot and you get an automatic response from certain specific members of the organism.[34]

The social Pavlovian nature of this procedure was, for Bernays, no exagger-
ation. Whether or not he and others could manipulate so mechanistically was
and is open to question, but Bernays claimed that he could:

effect some change in public opinion with a fair degree of accuracy by operating
a certain mechanism, just as the motorist can regulate the speed of his car by
manipulating the flow of gasoline.[35]

The way to reach that goal was by working on the leaders, and through them their followers, sometimes called "herds" by Bernays: "If you can influence the leaders, either with or without their conscious cooperation, you automatically influence the group which they sway."[36]

What Bernays proposed in *Propaganda*, and proudly argued in his 1928 article on "Manipulating Public Opinion," was nothing less than a new paradigm for public relations: Bernays' goal was to make a hero of "the special pleader who seeks to create public acceptance for a particular idea or commodity."[37]

For Bernays, public relations no longer needed to be defended as what sinful men do in a sinful society. Public relations would now be proclaimed as the service which saviors of that sinful society would take upon themselves to perform. It was hard work to be continuously "regimenting the public mind every bit as much as an army regiments the bodies of its soldiers," but someone had to do it.[38]

Who? Bernays vision of the future of public relations was most attractive to status-seeking practitioners. Certainly, Bernays wrote, "There are invisible rulers who control the destinies of millions." But those were not the political leaders or big businessmen of common paranoia. No, Bernays insisted that, "It is not generally realized to what extent the words and actions of our most influential public men are dictated by shrewd persons operating behind the scenes."[39]

The behind-the-scenes operators were necessary to the operation of a society, and there would not be that many of them: "The invisible government tends to be concentrated in the hands of the few because of the expense of manipulating the social machinery that controls the opinions and habits of the masses."[40]

As to the job description and title of behind-the-scenes operators, Bernays was precise:

> There is an increasing tendency to concentrate the functions of propaganda in the hands of the propaganda specialist. This specialist is more and more assuming a distinct place and function in our national life. [He] has come to be known by the name of "public relations counsel."[41]

Public relations counsels—leaders of the invisible government, taking upon themselves the responsibility of saving civilization from chaos. Public relations counsels—a brave new profession for a brave new world. "What we lack in this country now," he said near the close of our interview:

> are sound people who will pay no attention to the polls, and instead will apply the principles of social psychology to find out what the needs and wants of the

people truly are. Then those who understand public needs, including public relations counsels, will determine what democracy should give to the masses of the people. . . . Then they will explain these findings to the people, restating them in simple monosyllabic words with sentences no longer than 16 words. . . . Then the people will believe, our sacred dances will be intact, social chaos will be avoided, and public salvation will be here.[42]

CHAPTER NINE

The Triumph of Manipulation: Bernays Becomes Publicist No. 1

On the eve of the Depression, Bernays proclaimed his central message: Because "public opinion is slow and reactionary," those who use "the psychology of public persuasion . . . to bring about changes in public opinion" are performing a great public service.[1] Not until business executives felt hamstrung by public reaction to the NRA attempts, though, would they enthusiastically embrace a "public relations for the public interest" concept.

Acclaim came slowly to Bernays. When he first equated "manipulation of the public mind" with the "social purpose" of speeding change and preventing chaos,[2] not everyone knew what to make of it. Some reactions to his first book, *Crystallizing Public Opinion*, were enthusiastic. *The Bookman* called it, "A short but remarkably clear study. A book that every business man as indeed every artist should read."[3] *The Dial* also noted approvingly that the new book was not just about publicity, for:

> It is the larger aspects of this activity which concern Mr. Bernays . . . The book delves into psychology, ethics, salesmanship; it undertakes to show, in effect, how people may be divided into groups, how groups may be reduced to herds.[4]

Industry magazines such as the *Dry Goods Merchants Trade Journal* also took notice:

> No book has ever been written before taking up the idea of "public opinion." . . . How to influence an important individual, how to break up a hostile group by influencing a section of it, how to appeal to the entire mass – these are all prob-

lems that every man who is a leader in business today has confronting him constantly.[5]

Similarly, *Sales Management* commented that Bernays:

has written a very interesting book on the influencing of public opinion and the building of good will. When Napoleon said, "Circumstance? I make circumstance," he expressed very nearly the spirit of the work which must be done by a man who influences public opinion.[6]

At the end of some articles, though, a critical note often appeared. *The Survey* wondered about "the processes by which the herd instincts are exploited in the instincts of a new and far-ranging salesmanship."[7] *The Dial* had a line, "And with herds to play with, what may not the shepherd accomplish?"[8] Ernest Gruening, later to become a senator from Alaska, argued that:

This new sublimation is in response to an obvious need. Mr. Bernays points out that . . . "perhaps the most significant social, political, and industrial fact about the present century is the increased attention paid to public opinion," especially by men and organizations whose attitude not long ago would have been "the public be damned." Significant, no doubt. But, considering the nature of this attention, is it cause for rejoicing? Will the final result be greatly different for a public which, while it no longer tolerates being "damned," guilelessly permits itself to be "bunked"? Is seduction preferable to ravishment? . . . Mr. Bernays views the matter more rosily. His conclusion is that the public relations counsel is destined to fulfill his highest usefulness to society "in the creation of a public conscience." Not only may one doubt that the glorified press agent will fulfill this destiny, but that a public conscience thus "created" would be useful or desirable.[9]

There was evident concern about the potential power of the public relations practitioner.

Such criticism became heated after Bernays' publication in 1928 of his forthright book *Propaganda*, with its clear leanings toward subtly authoritarian "democracy." The reviewer in *Critic and Guide*, for instance, commented sarcastically about Bernays' "apparent – or well-assumed – sincere belief that he is doing some useful work" with "some real social value . . . "[10] Henry Pringle, in a 1932 issue of *The American Mercury*, commented wryly that, compared to Bernays, "Theodore Dreiser is a starry-eyed idealist. Eddie is a stern realist who operates on the demonstrable theory that men in a democracy are sheep waiting to be led to the slaughter."[11]

Inquiry magazine critiqued *Propaganda* with the suggestion "that we should be a whole lot better off if all propaganda were offered undisguised – that is, with full revelation of the promoting interests."[12] Leon Whipple, in *The Survey* of 1929, wrote of Bernays' apparent belief:

> that somebody 'who understands the mental processes and social patterns of the masses' should manipulate these controls so that people can know what to believe or buy. Society is too complex and folks too dumb to find out themselves. The counsel steps in to help – at a price. He rides here in a world of 'high-spotting,' fashion-making, window-dressing, blind instincts, and artifical habits, where events are created to make news, and indirection is the watch-word . . . The book is worth reading, for the Herr Doktor gives an almost metaphysical exposition of his creed . . . The general idea is to control every approach to the public mind so we get the desired impression, often unconsciously.[13]

The implications of Bernays' public relations paradigm also alarmed some political, academic, and religious observers during the 1930s, as concern about the political effects of mass manipulation (especially during economic downturn) became more widespread. For instance, in a 1934 letter to President Roosevelt, Justice Felix Frankfurter referred to Bernays and Ivy Lee as "professional poisoners of the public mind," exploiters of foolishness, fanaticism and self-interest.[14] Sociologist E. T. Hiller discussed Bernays' work and argued that "such widespread efforts to manipulate opinion constitute a financial burden, a perversion of intellectual candor, and a menace to political sanity."[15] The *Michigan Christian Advocate* noted that "there is danger in discovery of the mass mind" as advanced by Bernays.[16]

Journalists consistently criticized the effect of Bernaysian manipulation on information flow. Their perspective is well represented by frequent, sarcastic editorials in *Editor & Publisher* attacking Bernays' "new and higher ethics" and his "synthetic news creations." Editor Marlen Pew complained that Bernays' method is "to manipulate mass psychology and influence trade by propaganda so artfully insinuated into public consciousness that the victim does not realize that an unseen hand is leading him by the nose." Bernays, Pew wrote, tries "to sanctify propaganda as 'a vital social force.' But it is the same old dope." Pew called Bernays "my pick as the young Machiavelli of our time."[17]

A certain amount of economic jealousy was evident, of course. Newspapers prospered largely by selling advertising space. Publishers were concerned that free publicity for business might reduce demand for paid advertising. When *Editor & Publisher* labelled Bernays "the most modern, smoothest, highest paid and most effective of all the expert tribe of propagandists and spacegrabbers," the newspaper establishment clearly was reacting as an institution with monetary interests of its own.[18]

Still, both principal and principle were at stake. Bernays' pride in manipulating public opinion was diametrically opposed to the newspaperman's traditional (although perhaps naive) faith in reporting what happens and letting readers sort out the consequences. This larger question was never far beneath the surface of those frequent *Editor & Publisher* editorials: What happens to reportage based on the excitement of unpredictable events and free will at work, when more and more front page material happens not because of individual will but due to group preplanning?[19]

Bernays' own public relations also tended to suffer when comparisons were made between his techniques and those of the Nazis. One book in 1934, for instance, criticized the techniques of propaganda "carried to perfection by the Lord Northcliffes in wartime England, the Edward Bernays in industrial America, and the Dr. Goebbels in fascist Germany."[20] *Barrons* linked American and German-style public relations in 1935 when it noted that, "Hitler, by making what Bernays calls 'Devils' for the German masses to look down upon, has aroused the acclaim of the more easily swayed masses."[21] A magazine article in 1934 complained that Bernays was training "a new crop of manipulators of the public will," including, perhaps, "a new American Goebbels."[22]

Corporate employers of Bernays tossed off such criticism though, and Bernays' business increased rapidly following the NRA debacle of 1934, when corporate leaders realized that more subtle public relations would be necessary. The *Bulletin of the Financial Advertisers Association* examined profit figures in 1935 and then called Bernays "the outstanding counsel on public relations in the United States today, a profession he was largely instrumental in creating."[23] *Business Week* in 1937 noted that Bernays was able to understand "the mass mind, to reduce its workings to a scientific formula, to motivate its reactions." His ample retainer was a bargain because "He finds a direct way to mass minds through group leaders."[24]

Bernays' style was also appealing, as *The Commentator* in 1938 noted:

> Our striped-pants press agents of today don't brashly crash editorial gates. Their methods are more subtle. Edward Bernays, one of the most successful of the craft, can talk to his clients about human psychology with an expansiveness that would convince you of what he is, the nephew of Sigmund Freud; when he comes back for an encore you're puzzled as to whether or not he isn't Freud's uncle.[25]

Comments of those sorts are based on human toleration, but not professional admiration. The latter came to Bernays not just because he was successful, but because some saw him as successful in socially useful ways, which contributed to the holding back of chaos. For instance, an important book of the late 1930s, *Business Finds its Voice*, noted that large organizations seeking to overcome popular Depression antipathy needed new public relations methods to survive in order to perform their socially constructive activities.

Bernays had the secret: Far better "to implant an idea in a group leader's mind and let him spread it than to write up an idea and send it to the papers as a release, in the old-fashioned way . . . "[26]

Newsweek also was attracted by the hiddenness of persuasion: "One of Bernays' favorite symbols is the iceberg: What you see is big, but what you don't see is a lot bigger. Like the iceberg, much of Bernays' own work is invisible."[27] Even some highly-specialized publications caught on to the usefulness of the new methods and praised them; for instance, an article in *Etude*, a musicians' magazine, called Bernays,

> One of the most distinctive human products of our modern and highly complicated age . . . Press agents, or their equivalent, had existed since the early days of recorded history, but here was a new type, a scientist, applying all the latest discoveries in the social sciences to his task of gaining acceptance from the public for his client's products, enterprises and ideas.[28]

By the 1940s, according to *Current Biography* of 1942, Bernays had become "United States Publicist No. 1, head of a profession which he built up, publicized, and named: counsel on public relations."[29] Historians writing in 1942 were labeling Bernays "the ablest public relations man."[30]

By then, Bernays was moving to cement his approach by establishing it in colleges and universities. He was the first to teach a university course on public relations (at New York University in 1923). He wrote books and would write textbooks used in classrooms, and would develop the history of public relations which other textbooks would use in writing their own chapters on tradition and method. But he went one step further, as an *Advertising Age* article indicated:

> Bernays, often called "U.S. Publicist No. 1," has not only developed a far more profound concept of public relations, but has pioneered in establishing fellowships at American universities to carry forward the study of public relations. . . . It is Mr. Bernays' hope that from the studies of the men and women holding these fellowships will come 'a body of interpretative material which will help orient public relations thinking of the men in charge of our destinies in the postwar period.'[31]

Bernays' understanding of the importance of seizing the academies was another way in which he differed from earlier public relations practitioners. Bernays anticipated greater centralization in government and media, and the consequent growth of a new bureaucracy. He advocated governmental licensing of public relations counselors, or at the least a set pattern of formal, university training befitting those who would form a latter-day mandarin class.

Bernays also tried to enlist proponents of greater economic centralization in his public relations planning. Bernays did not try to hide his techniques and abilities from liberal critics. He was one of the first to realize fully that American 20th-century liberalism would increasingly be based on social control posing as democracy, and would be desperate to learn all the opportunities for social control that it could. In our interview, Bernays spoke highly of presidents whose programs led to greater governmental power. Bernays described himself as a political liberal and criticized those who thought that "public–private partnerships" would emerge without the behind-the-scenes manipulation that only sound public relations techniques could provide.[32]

Bernays showed his political philosophy clearly during the 1940s. In 1944, he paid for a series of full-page advertisements in *The Nation* and *The New Republic*, the two leading liberal magazines of the period, and later published the ads in a book entitled, *Plain Talk to Liberals*. The ads and book show the degree of similarity between Bernays and the left on the importance to "democracy" of economic planning and social control.[33]

Another short book Bernays published in 1945, *Take Your Place at the Peace Table*, was a clear appeal for a form of corporate socialism. Professor Pitman Potter, reviewing the latter book in the *American Political Science Review*, noted with some puzzlement that the book was "a mixture of honest liberalism and incipient cynical fascism." But that mixture was exactly what Bernays believed to be essential, given his understanding of the failure of 19th-century liberalism, and the 20th-century "necessity" of uniting liberalism with social control to avoid chaos.[34]

Potter made much sense in his specific criticisms. He noted that in Bernays' writing:

> There is much talk of the individual common man and open discussion and truth and accuracy, but much more of molding public opinion by various tools and weapons and plans and strategies, of swaying individuals and masses by powerful techniques of persuasion, by "the tested skills and practices of the professional public relations expert."[35]

Potter spotted the apparent contradiction in Bernays' theory on one page warning the reader that he was about to be duped, and on the next page providing specific instructions concerning the most effective ways of duping others.

Potter also noted that, for Bernays, means were subsidiary to ends: "If inaccuracy is to be abjured, it is—as far as we are told—only because it may provoke mistrust and loss of interest." Potter wrote that those means had been given a recent test: Bernays "presumably intends only welfare and happiness for humanity, but his methods are largely identical with those portrayed in Chapters VI and XI of *Mein Kampf*."[36]

What Potter did not understand, though, was that the contradictions apparent to a classically-trained political scientist formed a seamless web in the new world of public relations that Bernays was proposing. If the "individual common man" has no real individuality, as Bernays argued in *Propaganda* — only "rubber stamping" by one propagandist or another—then one more duping does no harm to individual souls.[37] And if Hitler had hit upon the techniques and used them for evil purposes, then that would be all the more reason—given the inevitability of these techniques being put into use and the inability of men to resist them—for liberals such as Bernays to use them before fascists had the chance.

Bernays suggested to his clients not only short-term maneuvers, but a long-term political agenda. As journalist Fulton Oursler put it, Bernays was successful because he could "apply the doctrines of his uncle, Sigmund Freud, to control the thinking of masses of people in behalf of big business, while advocating a kind of mild socialism of his own."[38] British political scientist J. A. R. Pimlott noted in 1951 that Bernays' writing "stood alone among works dealing specifically with public relations in having exerted any influence outside the narrow pubic relations world or much influence within it."[39] Daniel Boorstin called Bernays' writings "among the most sophisticated, philosophically self-conscious, and literate works on public relations."[40]

As we will see, those steeped in Bernaysian thinking worked during the post-NRA days to make corporations place public relations above private relations. Bernays' himself not only rode the wave of popular psychology and desire for social control, but also preached the inevitability of propaganda. A colorful comment from the show business newspaper *Variety* in 1960 may be the best testimony to his effectiveness: "Bernays did a book entitled *Propaganda* in 1928, but in those days propaganda was considered a rare form of word-racketeering. Today you can't see the truth for the slanted stories."

CHAPTER TEN

Public Relations
Adds Sugar

Until the Depression, industrial corporations (unlike the railroad, telephone, and electric utility companies) tended to be straightforward in their public relations work. Ivy Lee fought his way past some barriers and seeded companies with like thinkers, but it took the confluence of three streams – the agony of the economy, the failure of the NRA, and the thought of Bernays – to spread public-relations modernity through the Fortune 500.

The impending new era was signalled when Robert Lund, president of the National Association of Manufacturers, cited Bernays' work as proof that public relations should be carried out not only with announcements and press releases of Christmases past, but with "discretion and careful planning. . . ." Even though utility companies public-relations programs had been exposed, they provided examples of how "all channels through which the public may be reached must be used."[1]

One of Lund's first steps was to commission a nationwide public opinion poll to discover the most effective means of reshaping popular sentiment. He learned that many Depression-tired Americans were no longer interested in hearing about businessmen as entrepreneurial leaders, but saw business as a potential share-the-wealth arm of government. The initial public enthusiasm for the NRA reflected such thinking; and yet, the failure of the NRA showed that the idea, put into practice, was both unworkable and unpopular.

The public relations solution (pragmatic for some, ideological for those such as Bernays who had a long-term vision of American socialism) was to carry on covert NRA policies, including subtle price-fixing, and at the same time work to lead the American public into a long-term equation of government-corporate partnership with the public interest.

The new-style corporate messages that developed out of this consensus generally were soft-sell, or based on misdirection plays. General Motors, for instance, began portraying itself as a public servant, developing the theme, "Who Serves Progress—Serves America." United States Steel announced that its job was to create new products that would help Americans to avoid "despair." Du Pont had its famous slogan of "Better Things for Better Living." The National Association of Manufacturers aired a radio serial entitled, "The American Family Robinson," featuring friendly businessmen and characters such as Luke Robinson, "the sanely philosophical editor of the Centerville *Herald*" who wants a "fair deal for business and industry."[2]

The goal was subtlety. One of the best at achieving this goal was a former Bernays colleague, Carl Byoir. Byoir became expert at establishing front groups that could create "the impression of spontaneous grass-roots sentiment where none existed until his third party groups 'crystallized' it."[3] For instance, Byoir was hired by A&P in the late 1930s to mount a campaign against taxes on chain stores. As reporter Irwin Ross eventually discovered:

> Byoir and the A&P created—and paid the bills for—such presumably independent outfits as the National Consumers' Tax Commission, the Emergency Consumers' Tax Council and the Business Property Owners, Inc. This last group, headed by one Oscar E. Dooly, Jr., who was on Byoir's payroll, was so well camouflaged that not even the A&P's own field staff knew the whole story.[4]

In one sense, such activity was nothing new: railroads and utilities prepared ghostwritten articles and used professors, women's club leaders, and even the Boy Scouts to advance their cause. But Byoir & Associates went one step further when they created *new* organizations for their own purposes. A Byoir memo about a campaign begun in the 1940s concluded, "In sum, we not only have to create publicity ideas; we also have to go out in the field and create the groups and occasions so that those publicity ideas will become realities."[5]

What had started out as a search for public opinion quickly was transformed into an attempt to establish whatever public opinion suited those paying the bills. When confronted with the evidence of one manipulative scheme, Byoir manager Gerry Swinehart simply called his activity "group motivation," noting that "it's done all the time . . ."[6] By 1944, two public relations leaders could note in a *Public Opinion Quarterly* article that industry practice moved from "the public be damned" to "the public can be kidded."[7]

Some practitioners expressed concern over the change. In 1945 Rex Harlow, president of the American Council on Public Relations, expressed pride and concern about "an astronomical (sic) expansion of public relations activities. Almost everywhere one turns, one sees a new public relations counselor." But he worried that the goal for many of the new breed was to "pull the wool over the eyes of both the institution he represents and the public. Under this theory everybody is a sucker, to be played for all he is worth."[8]

Yet, Bernays' ideas about the public relations prevention of chaos appealed to many at the end of World War II. A survey in 1945 by the National Industrial Conference Board found "an attitude of complete acceptance of industry's responsibility for developing and maintaining good public relations. . . ."[9] In 1946 the Opinion Research Corporation found "a great surge of interest" in public relations, as 90% of companies surveyed increased their public relations budgets.[10]

Those in general management were being taught the Bernays gospel also. For instance, Dale Cox of International Harvester noted in 1949 that:

All the public relations men serving all American business . . . can't do the [public relations] job alone. It is too big. It has, therefore, to be the job of everyone in business, especially those in managerial capacities. . . . So, in our company, we are devoting as much attention now to the indoctrination and training of these managerial people in public relations as we do to the day-to-day operations [of the public relations department].[11]

Many individuals led the way toward a greater corporate public relations consciousness. At General Motors, Paul Garrett emphasized for over 25 years that partnership between government and business was inevitable. Arthur Page headed a public relations department in the Vail tradition at AT&T, gaining influence throughout industry by arguing that not only regulated utilities but all large companies should be treated as semi-public enterprises.[12]

The Committee for Economic Development (CED), established in 1942, became the key organization for instilling within management ranks both the methodology of soft-sell public relations and the long-term goal of government–business collaboration. What the CED stood for, according to one contemporary observer, was:

strangely indistinguishable from the content and outlook of the arguments of those who have long been pioneering methods of presenting the public relations case [for large corporations:] Ivy Lee, Edward L. Bernays, T. J. Ross [Lee's partner], Carl Byoir . . .[13]

Corporate public relations departments began trying to neutralize their political opposition not through principled argument but through the support of appealing cultural activities. Du Pont and other companies sponsored radio shows that would appeal to the historically-minded and, beginning in 1950, held annual "Educators Conferences" for potentially influential academics. Standard Oil of New Jersey (now Exxon) sponsored its own academic conference, the Jersey Roundtable, and produced a series of artistic films.[14]

Standard won friends in 1948 with its first full-length film, Robert Flaherty's *Louisiana Story*. (A fur company, Revillon Freres, sponsored the innovative documentary Flaherty filmed in 1922, *Nanook of the North*.) Flaherty took four years to make *Louisiana Story*, after receiving instructions that it was to be on "the search for oil" and include a human-interest story line. The film became the story of a Louisiana bayou family whose land was leased for oil exploration by Humble Oil Company. It was named the best documentary film of the year by the British Film Academy. Standard received high praise from critics for sponsoring a work of art.[15]

On the surface, civility helped to obscure deep divisions within industry ranks. Arguments concerning the extent of government-business collaboration were raging, but corporate public relations advisors advised that debates between company heads be kept from spilling out onto the street. The head of one of the largest public relations agencies, Earl Newsom, made the classic statement on this, telling his colleagues that the:

> cadence of statesmanship requires of you and me a certain discipline. We can help our bosses to avoid nasty, hotheaded reply when our institutions are criticized. We can help them to avoid public arguments. A battle of name-calling in the public press does not resolve issues and settle questions – it only creates public uncertainty and distrust of both parties. In this day of tensions – with the fear of the ultimate tension, atomic war, hanging over the heads of all of us – people are puzzled and distrustful when leaders of institutions serving them seem unable to resolve their differences privately.[16]

In the older style of private relations, internal company affairs were not the public's business, but differences between organizations were better settled out in the open, not behind closed doors with rumors of conspiracy circulating among those locked out. In modern public relations, though, the company's private enterprise would soon be an open book, whereas its public activities would be carried on in secret.

This upside-downness would be carried on in very sophisticated ways, however. As a public-relations woman, with the appropriate name of Constance Hope, admitted amusingly during the 1940s, the Bernays disciple:

> prepares impressive campaigns, studded with surveys, graphs, and excerpts from Freud, to show how he will mold the mass mind, psycho-analytically . . . The symbol of the Public Relations Counsel should be the whitewash brush, rather than the typewriter.[17]

Problems in ethics also were surfacing during this period. After all, if the goal of public relations was something as essential as the avoidance of chaos, then such an exalted end might justify virtually any means. By 1949 *Fortune* was proclaiming the triumph of public relations but noting that "no profession poses more ethical problems, even for its ablest people, than the practice of public relations."[18] A careful analyst of public relations, J. A. R. Pimlott, observed that "Lying may be said to be an occupational disease of public relations practice." One reason, he suggested, was that public relations, with its mix of financial incentive and Bernaysian ideal of control, had "drawn to its ranks a disproportionate number of those who delight in selling illusion."[19]

Many more magazine accounts of public relations ethical problems were published during the late 1940s and early 1950s, but the best analyses were often fond in the medium most concerned with character, the novel. Novels with public relations protagonists, and often written by public relations practitioners, began to appear in large numbers during the late 1940s and 1950s. Three novels in particular gave the flavor of life as societal savior, along with the ethical corollaries of that ideal.

In one, Robert van Riper's *A Really Sincere Guy*, a public relations practitioner who had long espoused free trade principles balks at developing a campaign for protectionism. His Bernays-type boss then tells him he has no rightful option, for:

> When you choose the profession of public relations counsel, you enter a very special calling. You acquire the tools and the skills to influence public opinion, and you [need . . .]flexibility, freedom from cumbersome convictions of one's own . . .[20]

In another, better-known novel, *The Man in the Gray Flannel Suit*, author Sloan Wilson has his hero join the public relations department of the "United Broadcasting Company." There he is brought into a plan based on "the newest maxim of the public relations boys" when an organization is under attack: Sidestep the charge by gaining a relatively inexpensive reputation for philanthropy.[21] In this instance, because United Broadcasting's television programs are being criticized:

> One thing the company could do is actually to improve the programs, but it would be cheaper to tell all the company's top executives, and particularly the president, to go out and acquire a reputation for doing good.[22]

The hero soon resigns.

A third and better novel, *Nobody's Fool* by Charles Harrison, has a major character apparently modeled on Bernays. The character explains that:

> Communications is the largest industry in the country . . . If you want the kind of civilization that gives you mass-produced cars, radios, and refrigerators, you've got to take what goes along with it. Everything, all the way down the line.[23]

He then advises the CEO of the "Iroquois Metals" company, threatened by attack from a Senator Marshlands, to:

> Go out and shop for a brand-new, spotless reputation for you and Iroquois Metals, so that when and if the Marshlands charges are made public they will sound utterly incredible. Now, follow me closely because this is how we're going to work this pitch. From here out you're going to stop being a tough, hardskinned industrialist. Overnight you're going to mature into a liberal, farsighted statesman of private initiative. Every time Marshlands or any other so-called liberal makes a speech in the Senate about how much he loves the common man, Iroquois Metals will applaud like crazy right out in the open. You will run full-page ads in papers all over the country [indicating that] Iroquois Metals and you as its president are dedicated to democracy and an era of abundance for the American people and that this advertisement is one of a public service series.
>
> After two or three months of that, anyone who says you were guilty of anything more than a mere technical violation of the election laws will be denounced in the liberal press as a dirty, red-baiting fascist stooge of the National Association of Manufacturers. There will be much more to the campaign than what I've just told you, but that's the gist of it. Do you get it?"
>
> I could see by the glittering, cunning quality of his eyes that he had quickly understood all the implications of the scheme. He had actually stopped eating; [he said], "Boy, you sure are a genius." I smiled, making no comment, taking a silent bow. Why should I tell him it was . . . an old trick and the professional magicians have always used it. Misdirection, they call it—something you do to divert the attention of the suckers while the undercover switcheroo is taking place. So, all right, I sure was a genius.[24]

The long-term effect of such short-term surcease, of course, could be dangerous: The Marshlands of the world would be built up, and Iroquois executives probably would start believing their own rhetoric. That is what tended to happen in the steel industry in real life, as the next chapter will show.

CHAPTER ELEVEN

Last Stand
For Steel

On April 10, 1962, U.S. Steel announced a general price increase; on April 13, it rescinded that increase after suffering denunciations from President John F. Kennedy and extra helpings of public scorn. Until 1962, some companies thought they could still engage in what could be called "private relations," that is, the making of business decisions without concentration on governmental or public opinion. After 1962, the importance of modern public relations was undisputed.

U.S. Steel's debacle is memorable for two reasons. It was a last stand for private relations; it also gave the American steel industry a hard push down its pathway to economic decline. Several articles and books have detailed the 72 hours of business–government tension in April, 1962.[1] What has been overlooked, though, is that U.S. Steel's attempt did not fail simply because it was outmaneuvered during those three days. If the battle of Waterloo was won on the playing fields of Eton, the last stand for private relations was lost, at least partly, because of three decades of steel industry public relations thinking preceding it.

The steel industry, after all, had often wanted governmental involvement in its pricing decisions. When the NRA was developing its wage and price controls in 1933 and 1934, many steel industry spokesmen were enthusiastic NRA backers. For instance, the trade magazine *Steel* favored the plan to "sacrifice certain rights" in order to gain "sanely coordinated activities." The managing director of the Steel Founders Society of America called the NRA an "inevitable step in social evolution." Armco Steel's George Verity praised the NRA as a "new sort of helpful partnership between government and business . . . We have accepted an entirely new philosophy."[2]

Some executives were explicit in their preference for expanded federal economic power. *Steel* magazine quoted the comment of a Republic Steel executive:

> We are not afraid of government intervention in business. If it corrects some of the long-standing evils in the steel business it will be doing something we have for years been trying unsuccessfully to accomplish for ourselves. We welcome this chance to put the entire industry on an equitable and ethical basis.[3]

Another industry leader, Bethlehem's Eugene Grace, praised the NRA's contribution to the "banishing of speculation in industrial prices." Grace thought price determination by factors of supply and demand too risky. He saw unfairness when a company was "confronted with the disturbing situation of having its entire financial structure continually at the mercy of negotiations between customer and salesman . . ." He preferred pricing by bureaucracy.[4]

After the Supreme Court declared the NRA unconstitutional in 1935, steel industry sentiments did not change greatly. Some 200 executives representing over 90% of the steel industry's productive capacity met following the Court's decision and unanimously resolved to continue abiding by the NRA code, but on a voluntary basis. They continued to praise the idea of government–industry collaboration to prevent lowered prices. But given the unpopularity of the NRA, they had to build public support for that concept.[5]

Public relations was essential. Bethlehem Steel expanded its public relations department (opened in 1930), U.S. Steel opened its own public relations department in 1936, and others followed suit. The American Iron and Steel Institute (AISI) established a public relations division. Steel industry public communications began to pour forth: 300,000 copies of a booklet, *Men Who Make Steel*; 3 million viewers of an AISI-produced film, *Steel*; an estimated 30 million readers of steel industry newspaper columns.[6]

The steel industry's new public relations organizations went beyond earlier industrial publicity in one crucial way: They not only attempted to increase the consumption of steel products, but also tried to make the public aware "that the sound functioning of the industry is a matter of vital public concern." The goal was to treat members of the public not as consumers of steel products but "participants" in the industry; steel companies henceforth would have not only stockholders, but "stakeholders," those who had been encouraged to see that they had a stake in industry success.[7]

AISI attempted to develop conscious stakeholders through increasing awareness of how and why major companies made decisions. It produced a monthly newsletter, *Steel Facts*, that was mailed to newspaper editors, college professors, and other influentials throughout the country. The Institute be-

gan circulating tracts containing speeches by steel executives on the importance of the "public interest," and gradually added additional publications.

AISI also hired a public relations firm, Hill and Knowlton. In the tradition
of Insull and the utility publicists of the 1920s, John Hill stressed "newspaper
publicity" and proposed to "enlist the active support and cooperation of the
editors." He and his firm did this through "friendly persuasion" and through
occasional attempts to link favorable coverage with advertising revenue.
When one Congressional committee produced proof of such practices, Hill's
associate Edgar Browerfind confessed but said his use of advertising pressure
to change news stories was a "mental aberration." Browerfind was not disci-
plined for this aberration.[8]

Throughout the late 1930s, the war years, and the late 1940s, the steel executives stressed their commitment to a broadly-defined public interest. This
becomes clear through a reading of speeches delivered at the AISI's annual
meetings during this period, and through an examination of statements contained in the annual report of the industry's flagship, U.S. Steel.

For instance, at the 1939 meeting at the Waldorf-Astoria in New York,
Chairman Arthur Roeder of Colorado Fuel & Iron suggested that the industry's most important task was not to produce more, but to "obtain the good-
will of the outside world." This could be accomplished only if industry leaders:

> show America that we are not living by worn-out rules, but with the full con-
> sciousness of our new social responsibilities, brought about by consistently
> changing standards.[9]

Even though standards were changing fast, industry leaders would have to
rush to keep up with them, because a corporation's job was to acquiesce:
When there was "deviation of the corporate policy from the public interest,"
Roeder said, a company that wanted "sound public relations" would move to-
wards "alignment."[10]

World War II offered the steel industry an opportunity for improved public
relations. Edward Ryerson, chairman of Inland Steel, noted at the 1944 annual meeting:

> We have several factors in our favor, resulting from the war activities . . . We
> find the greatest opportunity that has ever existed whereby a vital industry can
> be made a matter of great public interest.[11]

By the 1946 annual meeting, AISI leaders were claiming success for their
post-NRA plan to increase public interest in the steel industry. AISI President
Walter S. Tower spoke of "contrasts between the pre-Code Institute and what
it is today": paid AISI staff increased from 15 to 44; AISI volunteer commit-

tees increased from 12 (with 66 members) to 50 (with 500); millions of publications were being distributed. Tower said the massive public relations thrust grew out of NRA collaboration: "The experience of working together under the Code gave steel men a new concept of what legitimate cooperation can do for an industry."[12]

Ryerson of Inland Steel became chairman of the Institute's Committee on Public Relations. He announced at the 1947 annual meeting that millions of publications, advertisements, radio messages, and other activities, were designed to propagate the steel industry message of company conformity to the public interest.

The "heart of our message," Ryerson said, was the steel industry performance of a "service at a fair price and fair profit with a high degree of economic efficiency and a deep sense of responsibility." If Ryerson's ideas of public relations effectiveness were correct, millions of Americans were coming to believe that "our" steel industry existed to serve "the nation," and that only prices and profits perceived as "fair" should be allowed.[13]

In this medieval, "just price" conception of economics, the nation legitimately would have a large role in deciding what was fair, so public relations would be essential. Hiland Batcheller, chairman of Allegheny Ludlum Steel Corporation, told the 1950 annual meeting that the industry's chief need was not better research, production or marketing: "The thing this industry needs more than anything else is men who know how to talk." Batcheller recommended the hiring of "top executives" who would concentrate on "making friends" and "spend more time in Washington talking with newsmen and government officials . . ."[14]

U.S. Steel, the largest steel producer, was also the industry's largest public relations producer. Top corporate leaders spent much of their time on public relations from the 1930s onward. Even Bernays was surprised at the executive efforts, noting with astonishment in his autobiography that "a large part of U.S. Steel Chairman Edward Stettinius' job in 1940 was supervision of a movie about the making of steel."[15]

Once Stettinius joined the Roosevelt–Truman administrations and became Secretary of State, his successor, Irving Olds, noted in the company's 1945 annual report "the emphasis in U.S. Steel" on attainment of "favorable public opinion . . ."[16]

Year after year, a special section of U.S. Steel's annual report laid out the ways in which the public was being pleased. The 1949 annual report told of the company's 5-year sponsorship of 185 Sunday evening broadcasts of The Theatre Guild on the Air radio program, its sponsorship of NBC radio network concerts, its making of a technicolor motion picture to dramatize the impact of stainless steel, and its distribution of books about the industry to schools and colleges.[17]

In 1950, the annual report stated that U.S. Steel, through its radio program sponsorship and its distribution of speeches and pamphlets, was making "greater headway than ever before in creating a better general understanding of the constructive role it is playing in the lives of the American people."[18]

Public relations victory seemed within grasp during the 1950s, according to U.S. Steel's annual reports. Stockholders could learn that, "During 1954, U.S. Steel reached the highest public acceptance in its 53-year history," judging by Psychological Corporation (Link Audit) analysis. The following year news was even finer: "As an indication of increasing public acceptance of U.S. Steel and its policies, the Link Audit showed that U.S. Steel in 1955 had earned an all-time high in 'good-will profit.' " "Public acceptance" was a heading in every U.S. Steel annual report of the 1950s.[19]

U.S. Steel's "good-will profit" seemed to have two causes. The 1956 annual report noted that "an especially sharp gain in public acceptance began two years ago at the time U.S. Steel entered the field of television with the dramatic series, *The United States Steel Hour*." Another report argued that:

In the past year, the connection between the presentation of high quality visual entertainment and the increasing public confidence in U.S. Steel, and the furthering of its commercial aims, was clearly apparent.[20]

Throughout the decade, annual reports suggested that television sponsorship of well-regarded shows created for the company what those in the public relations trade call a halo effect.

A deeper cause of apparent good will, though, may have been the care which U.S. Steel executives took to avoid angering anyone – in particular, competitors, employees, and government officials.

Competitors were not angered because U.S. Steel led other major producers in the maintenance of a covert NRA through the use of subtly administered pricing. In 1961 M. A. Adelman of the Massachusetts Institute of Technology discussed this brilliantly:

The process of price increases had been a striking spectacle. Between March and July, the industry has staged a yearly ritual – one might call it the rites of spring, only it is far more sedate than anything Igor Stravinsky ever thought of orchestrating. First, a steel company issues a statement that the price of steel "should" by rights be raised . . . because only by raising prices can the industry raise enough money to provide investment in the new steel capacity . . . A drop-off in demand for steel is not only no obstacle, but actually a help, since it raises unit "costs" and thereby makes a price increase all the more "justified."[21]

Adelman pointed out that U.S. Steel's rationale for price increases "plainly assumes a monopolistic industry – it is strongly reminiscent of a regulated public utility." The result was that, from 1947 to 1957, prices for all goods rose by an average of 2% per year, but steel prices rose by an average of 7%. Inefficient competitors did not have to tighten up or drop out. Hard feelings did not arise.[22]

Labor harmony also prevailed, with wages increasing during the 1947–1957 decade by about 7% each year, compared to a 2% inflation rate. The United Steelworkers Union was firmly established as the voice of all blue-collar employees within the industry. It could call on powerful allies in the White House (during the Truman administration) and Congress if negotiations should prove sticky. But, until 1959, with one exception (in 1951), there was little need for threats, as a continuation of demand for domestic steel products seemed guaranteed.

There were a few rough moments in the steel industry's governmental relations. During the late 1940s and early 1950s federal officials wanted the steel industry to increase capacity; governmental economists felt that if demand for steel did increase sharply and the industry was not ready, bottlenecks affecting the entire economy would develop. In his January, 1949, State of the Union message, President Truman even suggested that Congress should authorize the construction of state-owned facilities if private enterprise did not undertake construction.[23]

The steel industry attitude was different. Some industry leaders knew of the pressure to increase capacity after World War I, amid expectations of soaring demand; at the end of 1921, though, steel production was at only 33% of capacity. Many knew that capacity utilization had fallen below 20% during the Depression, and feared similar problems. Republic Steel's 1947 annual report contended that capacity increases "are not warranted today."[24]

U.S. Steel was particularly critical of demands to expand capacity. The 1946 annual report pointed out, "In years of peace, U.S. Steel has used from as little as two-tenths to as much as nine-tenths of its capacity to produce steel." The 1948 annual report argued that unnecessary capacity expansion would merely result in "higher prices for steel products . . . in order to provide an adequate return on the huge investment needed for these proposed large mills." In the 1951 annual report U.S. Steel cited steps it had taken to increase capacity following the outbreak of the Korean War, but continued to resist the doubling of capacity some called for, since national defense needs were taking only ⅛ of steel industry production.[25]

At first, industry executives testified regularly that dramatic increases in capacity were unnecessary. Ernest T. Weir, chairman of the National Steel Corporation, told the House Judiciary Committee that:

> There has never been a steel shortage under normal conditions in my experience. The steel industry had always had capacity exceeding current demand . . .

In the past fifty years, the public requirement for steel has amounted to an average of only 70% of steel capacity.[26]

The Supreme Court was also on the side of the industry. When President Truman in 1951 tried to force the issue of steel production by temporarily seizing steel mills, the Supreme Court ruled his action unconstitutional.

But the steel industry, in fighting demands for overexpansion, was risking public furor and apparently going back on its own public interest rhetoric; after all, if the steel industry was really a national public service, then on what basis could demands by the nation's elected leaders for capacity expansion be resisted?

In this case, the demands were not resisted. Trapped by their own rhetoric and scared by presidential threats, U.S. Steel executives and others rejiggered expansion plans to meet demands for greater public service. Overall, industry capacity expanded by 62% from the end of World War II through 1959, up to 149 million net tons. The greatest expenditures for capacity expansion came in 1952, the year after President Truman's temporary nationalization. Rushed expansion continued until the latter part of the decade.

With happy labor relations and expansive public relations, the industry's "good will profit" during the mid-1950s was at an all-time high. Demand for steel seemed "highly inelastic," and "increasing evidence of potential entry" was ignored. U.S. Steel Chairman Benjamin Fairless in 1956 continued to stress the importance of "harmony," contending that:

> The trouble with the oldtime management was that it was just a little too individualistic . . . Modern management, with its professional attitudes, its concern for the public welfare and public relations and generally humane attitudes toward business, is far better than the old system . . . today's 'man in the gray flannel suit' is ten times more efficient than his more colorful, more hot-tempered predecessor.[27]

Public relations had created a glow of satisfaction even inside the industry.

By the end of the 1950s, though, it was clear that the industry experts had been right to resist capacity expansion; the governmental economists had been wrong. Domestic steel consumption grew at a rate of only 0.4% throughout the 1950s. The original industry plan for slow expansion would have been perfect.

The result of fast expansion, however, was a huge capacity increase in what was essentially a flat market: With consumption growing at 0.4% per year, capacity was growing ten times as fast, at a compound annual rate of over 4%. This had an obvious effect on operating rates, which averaged 89% for 1951–55 but only 73% for 1955–60.

Furthermore, the pressure for rapid capacity expansion had led to a decision to go for "more" rather than "better." As Barnett and Schorsch, probably the best economic analysts of steel problems, have pointed out:

> During the 1950s, investment was generally of the capital-widening rather than capital-deepening type—that is, funds were devoted primarily to additional productive units embodying familiar technology rather than to the adoption of new technologies. Thus, the investments that fueled the expansion of steel-making capacity failed to incorporate major technological breakthroughs.[28]

The expansion was in open hearth furnaces. Under governmental pressure, against the recommendations of the technical experts, money was sunk into such facilities.

Several problems resulted. First, even without new technological developments, that unneeded capacity would have been a white elephant, eating up corporate resources and cutting into profits usable for future investment. Second, the open hearth technology was becoming uncompetitive even as it was installed, as the basic oxygen furnace approach was demonstrably more efficient. *Business Week* in 1963 would characterize the capacity-building program of the 1950s as "40 million tons of the wrong kind of capacity—the open-hearth furnace."[29]

The open-hearth expansion of the early- and mid-1950s, if postponed for several years, could have been an oxygen furnace expansion, which would have allowed the American steel industry to remain profitable. The poorly-timed expansion could be characterized as bad luck—an attempt at goodness gone wrong, but goodness had nothing to do with it. Those capacity increases that wasted billions of dollars and eventually led to large unemployment resulted from an overruling of technical expertise by industry executives pressured by federal bureaucrats.

It would later become possible to point fingers at governmental economists for producing mistaken projections of demand growth. Yet, it must be noted that the steel industry, ideologically weakened from within by its desire for public involvement in its activities and its goal of "good-will profit," did not put up much of a fight. The economic results included a:

> steady erosion of operating rates, as new capacity came onstream while demand remained essentially flat. . . . Even robust growth in demand would not have saved the industry's open hearths from technological obsolescence by the mid-1960s. Had steel capacity grown only with demand, however, the inevitable transition to the basic oxygen furnace would have been eased. A more sober, conservative, and realistic investment strategy would have saved the industry much of the anguish connected with the abandonment of the open hearth.[30]

Further problems were starting to arrive ahead of schedule during the late 1950s. The *Wall Street Journal* regularly began printing tidbits such as the following:

> Italian-fabricated steel transmission towers will begin arriving in New York shortly for assembling along a 150-mile New York Power Authority Line between Niagara Falls and Syracuse, New York. Akron's Goodyear Tire and Rubber Company and Firestone Tire and Rubber Company have turned to France and Belgium for certain types of wire for tire reinforcing. Borg-Warner Corporation of Chicago is experimenting with foreign steel, and finding the metal 'up to domestic quality.'[31]

Industry executives perceived the growing problem. *Time* magazine quoted the wail of Thomas F. Patton, president of Republic Steel:

> First the foreign manufactures took our foreign market. Then they went after our coastal market. Now they're invading our inland market. Everyone in the industry feels that foreign steel is a growing menace.[32]

After a decade of talking harmony, steel executives began to see that they had a hard fight on their hands, with no end in sight.

This was a startling development. Ever since the NRA days, it seemed that as long as American steel companies kept from fighting among themselves, kept unions happy, and gave the public a sense of participation in the industry, almost everyone could be satisfied. Now, a turn-around was necessary; if everyone could not be satisfied, hard choice among private interests would have to be made. Would the public, petted for a quarter century and told it was master, sit still for this? Would steel industry executives, taught that the bad old days of individualism were behind them, have the will to fight?

The first part of the belated drive to break out of harmony came in regard to unions. Industry executives saw that, with a Republican president unlikely to take the union's side, 1959 might be a good time to let marketplace pressures decide wages. U.S. Steel decided to take a strike, in the hope that public relations pressure would help it obtain a better settlement than could be obtained by the continued pursuit of harmony through soft settlement.

Curiously, despite all of its public relations work and good-will profit, U.S. Steel found that public opinion was not on its side during the strike. The public that had been taught to regard the steel industry as "our" industry, a public trust abiding by public opinion, took that sentiment seriously and began demanding a settlement in the public interest. U.S. Steel public relations had suggested to the public that price and wage decisions were based on "fairness," not market demands. The public was now saying that "fairness" required a higher wage, one the companies could give because they (supposedly) could get it back through higher prices.

The sudden stiffening on wages by U.S. Steel and other companies ran counter to two decades of peace at any wage. Suspicion was rampant. Adelman observed, "If the companies were now unwilling to give more, their true reason must (therefore) be something hidden, therefore sinister: say, destruction of the union."[33]

That was not the real reason: Industry leaders had seen the darkness at the end of the tunnel and knew that they quickly had to become competitive with foreign steel. But, after all the years of harmony-praising public relations, their attempt to put the publicity engines in reverse was not successful. Neither union nor public accepted the newly dire forecasts, and the Eisenhower administration eventually bent also. A compromise settlement was arranged, with wages going up sharply once more.

The second part of the attempted breakout came three years later, in April, 1962. U.S. Steel executives, now aware that their capacity expansion of the previous decade was merely leading to greater inefficiencies and competitive weakness, resolved on a crash program of investment in new technology. Having spent their cash for old technology, though, they needed to raise more money for oxygen furnaces and other new developments. Still having to pay out more in wages, they resolved on trying to get more revenue for investment by raising prices.

In the face of foreign competition and anticipated hostile public reaction, this was a desperate choice, but U.S. Steel Chairman Roger Blough and other executives saw no alternative. They were willing to give up some short-term market share in return for a long-term answer to international competition. "For the sake of his company, the industry, and the nation, Blough sought a way to break through the bland 'harmony' that has recently prevailed between government and business," *Fortune* noted. As columnist Charles L. Bartlett observed, Blough's:

> previous attempts to combine politics and business in the Eisenhower administration were not notably profitable for his company, and he appears to have determined to act at this time in pure business terms.[34]

To act in "pure business terms": This was a drastic change from a half-century of U.S. Steel as "semipublic enterprise." So prevalent had public-relations-thinking become at U.S. Steel that its former chairman, Myron Taylor, had complained of his difficulty in finding individuals "who will leave private business and devote themselves to the corporation."[35]

Nevertheless, U.S. Steel's economic prospects became so troubled that even its public relations vice president, Phelps Adams, "fully concurred in the proposed price action." As he told one interviewer:

> I counseled in favor of the action. In doing so, I fully realized – as did the other executives of the company – that a price increase would be highly unpopular and would create some problems both in Washington and with the public generally, but in the light of the economic circumstances, which were also fully discussed, it seemed to me that the price action was the proper course to take . . . [36]

Blough and Adams knew that public reaction would be harsh. For one thing, large steel companies, with help from the Kennedy administration, had just completed new labor agreements with the United Steelworkers. The agreements provided for substantial wage increases, but the industry had come out somewhat better than it had three years before. Even though U.S. Steel had never stated or implied an agreement not to raise prices, it was predictable that some officials would be mad.

Blough and Adams did not anticipate the full fury of governmental and public reaction. At a specially-called press conference, President Kennedy publicly attacked the increases as "a wholly unjustifiable and irresponsible defiance of the public interest." From the 1930s through the 1960s U.S. Steel's public relations department had grown from 4 to 179, with most of those employees busy saying that U.S. Steel's job was to serve the public; when the public's elected representative, the President of the United States, said that the company was acting against the public interest, and when 77% of the public agreed with him, what could Roger Blough do?[37]

Just in case U.S. Steel would continue to hang tough, the Kennedy administration played hardball. Personal income tax returns of steel executives and their expense accounts were dug out. When several other large steel companies also seized the opportunity to raise prices, newspaper reporters who had heard previous executive comments opposed to increases were awakened in the middle of the night and asked to produce their notes. Privately, Kennedy said that his father had told him that all steel executives were "sons of bitches." (This was later reported as Kennedy's famous "all businessmen are sons of bitches" statement, apparently a misquotation.)[38]

Most crucially, Administration supporters jawboned leaders of smaller steel companies; when several announced that they would not increase prices, additional pressure on U.S. Steel and other large steel makers was enough to force a turnaround. U.S. Steel rolled back its prices amidst increasing criticism.

Those who associated governmental power with a triumphant "public interest" cheered U.S. Steel's defeat. Walter Lippmann attacked U.S. Steel for having tried to raise prices "without previous notice to or consultation with anyone speaking for the national interest." The New York *Times* editorialized:

> The forces of our democracy scored a dramatic triumph last week when the major steel companies bowed to the storm of both governmental and public protest and rescinded the price increases they had decreed.[39]

Some on the political right, though, criticized the Kennedy administration's public pressure and private strongarm tactics. Columnist David Lawrence wrote that:

> A new era in American history – a declaration of war by the government on the profit system as it functions under private capitalism – has been ushered in by President Kennedy.[40]

Senator Barry Goldwater, preparing to run for president in 1964, argued that Kennedy's attack was "something you'd expect in a police state." William E. Robinson, recently retired president of Coca-Cola, asked in a letter to former president Eisenhower, "What now about the free enterprise system . . . when [Kennedy] denies the right of a business to price its goods?"[41]

There were scattered protests from the steel industry, particularly from executives in small companies. E. B. Germany, president of Lone Star Steel Company, said:

> Using tactics never before assumed by an Administration in peacetime, the President assumed the role of prosecutor, judge, and jury, to bring unprecedented influences to bear upon the steel industry. He assumed dictatorial powers when he directed that Government purchases of steel be made from companies which did not increase prices.[42]

Republic Steel President Thomas F. Patton gave a drier account at his annual stockholders meeting on May 9, 1962:

> Efforts at persuasion by a government official should not be accompanied by grand jury actions, visits from agents of the Federal Bureau of Investigation, the cancelling of government steel orders, and investigation by committees of Congress.[43]

The prevalent tone, however, was one of acceptance. Whether governmental officials *should* deny businesses the right to price their goods seemed no longer the question; it was now firmly understood that officials *could*, and *would*. One analyst of public relations, Lou Golden, concluded after U.S. Steel's defeat that:

The lessons for corporations are clear and unmistakable. They cannot function without public consent. To obtain that consent they must act in the public interest as the public interprets it at any given time. . . . True, the public interest is not easy to define. And what the public interprets as being in its interest may change a week from next Wednesday morning.[44]

It was commonly believed among public relations practitioners that there could now be no alternative to attempts at riding that public interest whirlwind. Denny Griswold wrote in *Public Relations News*, a trade newsletter: "The nation's press almost unanimously has condemned the company as have practically all the PR professionals with whom we have discussed the subject."[45]

Blough himself made it clear, following his defeat, that he would make no more attempts to resurrect private relations. Three months after the debacle, he posed the question, "Are we doing everything we can to increase the government's confidence in business?" He then answered it: A "cooperative spirit" leading to "mutual action and mutual understanding in our time" was essential.[46]

The Kennedy Administration welcomed this desire for government-business peace in our time. A July, 1962, memo to Kennedy by aide Theodore Sorenson recommended a series of dinner meetings with business leaders; Sorenson noted, "Any steps taken for the primary purpose of pleasing the business community should be largely psychological, not substantive." Kennedy followed that advice by holding an informal White House question-and-answer session for 60 executives in December, 1962.[47]

At the session, Kennedy had nothing substantive to say; as historian Kim McQuaid noted, this was a "ritual observance. The President of the United States was taking time out from his killing schedule to chat politely and informally . . ." But, crucially, Roger Blough introduced Kennedy to the assembly: "The symbolism of the two former adversaries in the steel struggle standing cheek by jowl over cocktails was surely lost on no one." All was forgiven as long as public relations was embraced.[48]

Blough, beaten, did his part. During the Johnson–Goldwater presidential race of 1964, when Scripps–Howard interviewers asked Blough about government-business relations, Blough replied, "You might say, 'Never the twain shall meet.' I say the opposite. The twain have to meet continuously if government and business are to perform their functions properly." During an October 7, 1964, speech in Chicago, Blough stressed "a new and developing attitude of cooperation between government and business . . ."[49]

The battle was over. The 1962 steel crisis was private relations' last stand. The attempt by Roger Blough and his associates to reverse three decades of public relations dominance was too little, too late.

CHAPTER TWELVE

Governmental Relations and Contributions Policies, 1962–1982

Corporate executives had the opportunity to learn from the U.S. Steel debacle in two ways: by concentrating on *what* happened and by analyzing *why* it happened. Many reporters and public relations managers told of the action itself: A public fight culminating in a black eye for business. The 30-year buildup to the scrape generally was ignored. Public relations leaders, skipping by the *why*, drew a convenient moral for those who had paid attention only to the *what*: They argued that a larger public relations presence in Washington, and greater attempts to keep federal officials happy, would avoid similar problems. Some, such as Bernays, suggested that the long-run solution was government-business partnership.[1]

The first general opportunity to act on lessons learned, one way or the other, came as the 1964 election campaign approached. The Republican candidate, Barry Goldwater, had condemned strongly Kennedy administration interference with U.S. Steel's pricing decisions. He received support during his campaign from executives of Eli Lilly, Quaker Oats, and a handful of other large companies. But the "National Independent Committee for President Johnson and Senator Humphrey" enlisted 3 thousand CEOs, including Henry Ford II, Thomas Lamont of the Morgan Guaranty Trust, John Loeb of Loeb, Rhoades and Company, Frederick Kappel of AT&T, Sol Linowitz of Xerox, Kenneth Adams of Philips Petroleum, Ralph Lazarus of Federated Department Stores, and John Connor of Merck and Company, who would become Johnson's Secretary of Commerce.[2]

Archives of the Presidential Library show that Johnson worked hard for such support, dispatching his assistants to bird-dog key executives and file regular reports. For instance, a January, 1964, memo from aide Mac Kilduff to Jack Valenti discussed "the impression which the President has made on Mr. Kappel [of AT&T] . . . with a little more attention Kappel might come out in favor of the President."[3] Kappel received the attention and announced his support. Similarly, library archives reveal how Johnson flattered executives, as in a September, 1964, note to Henry Ford II that called him "a bellweather in the nation. Where you go, less courageous souls are willing to follow."[4]

Because the ideological base for supporting Johnson's concept of a Great Society public-private partnership was established during the NRA days and added to since then, it took little courage for corporate executives to follow. The *New York Times* in August, 1964, estimated that 60% of the members of the Business Council, a key group of major corporate executives, planned to vote for Johnson. Johnson received 61% of recorded contributions from Business Council members.[5]

Those who had not followed trends in corporate public-relations thinking were surprised. Liberal commentator David T. Bazelon concluded that "a startlingly significant vanguard of the corporate barons" were part of a "serious institutional and political approach to Washington."[6] But Marion Folsom, a former Eastman Kodak executive and Secretary of Health, Education, and Welfare, simply noted that many executives had come to see governmental action as "the right way of doing things."[7]

Following the Johnson election, large corporations increased their hiring of liberal politicians and political aides who could both lobby in Washington and teach the new ways to any executives who remained recalcitrant. For instance, General Motors hired Theodore Sorenson, who had told President Kennedy following the steel crisis that superficial stroking would make businessmen feel better. The *Harvard Business Review* in 1967 noted that executives had "actively embraced the idea of the interventionist state" and were showing "a remarkably tolerant and friendly attitude toward the complex congeries of national fiscal, monetary, and social welfare policies inaugurated during Mr. Johnson's first three years as President."[8]

The following year, as the strains of Vietnam began to bring down the Johnson administration, key executives were still strong in their support. Federal deficits increased as the budget was battered partly by military expenditures but mainly by fast-growing Great Society costs; Johnson's business supporters offered to lobby for a tax increase. Following a 2-hour meeting with Johnson at the White House on August 10, 1967, corporate leaders such as Henry Ford II, Kappel, Walter Wriston of Citibank, Albert Nickerson of Mobil, Thomas Gates of Morgan Guaranty Trust, Rudolph Peterson of the Bank of America, David Rockefeller of Chase Manhattan, and Stuart Saunders of Penn Central, joined with Werner Gullander, president of the National Association of Manufacturers, and Allen Shivers, president of the U.S.

Chamber of Commerce, to form a committee for a tax surcharge. Five hundred CEOs added their names to the list.[9]

This was an amazing turn of events to observers who had not kept up with changing business ideologies. Some officials predicted that corporate executives would oppose tax increases; they could not believe that the business leaders were sincere. White House aide Harry McPherson told Joseph Califano late in October, 1967, that corporate support for the tax increase was part of a cynical strategy that assumed Congress would not go along:

> Businessmen and bankers are supporting you on the surtax so that they will feel free to increase prices and interest rates after you lose the surtax fight . . . They will have fought the good fight, and it will be Congress' fault, not theirs, when the next round of inflation comes.[10]

If that was the original intention, it did not survive once corporate public and governmental relations department enthusiastically put their shoulders to the wheel. One memo to Johnson explained that hesitant congressmen were being pressured by "company representatives who are either headquartered or who have important plant operations in the District of the individual House member."[11] On June 28, 1968, the tax surcharge was passed.

Short-term public relations reasons for backing Johnson on the surcharge issue were evident: Johnson personally was pleading, and supportive corporations would have his administration's IOUs. Ironically, Johnson was the lamest of lame duck presidents by the time the surcharge was passed. Winning his gratitude did not count for much. For some executives, though, the long-term strategy was more important: Increasingly, corporate public-relations leaders were ideologically committed to a close government-business partnership, with the Bernaysian goal of avoiding chaos. As Kappel's successor as CEO at AT&T, H. I. Romnes, told the Wisconsin Manufacturers Association flatly in 1966, corporations will be part of "a future in which the public and private sectors will become more and more intertwined."[12]

Nor were executives offering tribute to such concepts only during liberal Democratic administrations. In 1971, Richard Nixon won temporary support from those favoring greater governmental power by announcing a 90-day wage-price freeze, with the prospect of some controls afterwards as well. As in the days of the NRA, corporate leaders applauded the governmental action. Gabriel Hauge, chairman of Manufacturers Hanover bank, said Nixon has "lanced the boil of pessimism." Arch Booth, executive vice president of the U.S. Chamber of Commerce, said he favored the freeze and thought that longer-run wage and price controls could "achieve stability." The National Association of Manufacturers agreed that the controls could "advance the economic well-being of the nation . . ."[13]

Once again, there were points to be won with the Administration, but other benefits too. Wage and price controls could stymie union demands. The prospects for Soviet and Chinese trade fascinated executives looking for old worlds to conquer. Protectionists applauded Nixon's 10% surcharge on imports and his adoption of floating exchange rates that lowered the value of the dollar against major foreign currencies. A government-created election-eve economic boom also showed executives that playing the Washington game could be profitable. As Secretary of Defense Melvin Laird later related, "Every effort was made to create an economic boom for the 1972 election. The Defense Department, for example, bought a two-year supply of toilet paper."[14] Toilet paper manufacturers were ecstatic.

Above all, some executives were learning that it was easier to make a profit in the air-conditioned corridors of Washington than by selling goods to customers, one by one, on mean and dusty streets. When the freeze was lifted, prospective price increases were in the hands of an erratic 15-member Price Commission that could single out one company for stinging public condemnation while smiling sweetly at similar antics by another. The game became collaboration, making friends with Washington regulators to protect a company's interests. Even executives and public relations practitioners who hated the new rules often found that they had to pay for the sins of their predecessors.

There were a few minor drawbacks, of course. Inflation rose to an 11.5% annual rate during the last quarter of 1972. The following year brought a plethora of after-dinner speeches about the need for spending reductions and tight money policies, but during working hours corporate jockeying for position intensified. Business decisions—who to hire or fire, what to use for fuel, what to charge for goods—were now being made not by private enterprise but by government, in the public interest, of course.

Given the public relations campaign of "business in the public interest" that began during the 1930s, corporate executives could oppose regulatory excesses only by saying that their conception of the public interest was different. But business leaders were unelected, so how could they know the public better than those officially designated as public servants? Besides, most CEOs were unphotogenic.

Throughout the 1970s, therefore, many of the largest corporations collaborated on the writing of new regulations, and helped to construct them in a way that harmed smaller competitors while offering king-size loopholes. Political veterans were hired to work this "loophole lobby." Increasingly, there was not even a pretense of free market thinking among many Washington representatives, many of whom had "spent their formative professional years being nurtured by the redistributionist philosophy of Washington."[15] As one *Wall Street Journal* column noted, many governmental relations staffers believe that:

wealth creation is an irrelevant if not suspect activity. Too often they accept an apologetic or defensive stance whenever their industry is attacked, and are willing to plea-bargain early on. For them, compromise is always preferable to resistance. The Washington rep often focuses on what 'improvements' and 'perfecting' amendments can be made to bills whose sole intent is to further shackle business, rather than on seeking to defeat such measures. Such tactics, of course, ensure continued losses.[16]

It's not just the governmental relations specialists who were acting that way. Such thinking was evident in other sectors of corporate public relations as well. Many corporate contributions programs, for instance, originally were seen as a way to aid educational institutions that train future employees. Some stockholders objected to such nonbusiness expenditures, but the New Jersey Supreme Court, in *A. P. Smith Manufacturing Company v. Barlow* (1953), gave its blessing by noting that private enterprise was benefitting from the contributions.[17]

In the 1960s, however, companies looking for political allies began going far beyond economic education and contributions to universities. Some nervously dipped a toe into the waves of social reform surfed on by Great Society planners. The "community relations" contributions custom was soon so well established that even Roger Blough, defeated in his battle with the Kennedy administration, found it necessary to take time away from minding the store.

Blough was typical in his 1960s pledge to help "big business to discharge fully its obligations as a corporate citizen of the community . . . to contribute both time and money to civic improvements, charity drives, hospitals, schools and recreation facilities."[18] In 1967 *Look* magazine reported that the newly-developed, benign impulses of oligarchs were transforming them from "blue chip chiefs, drawing $40 to $252 an hour," into "a bunch of social workers."[19]

The rhetoric of social responsibility escalated throughout the 1970s. By the early 1980s, some companies were publishing contributions "annual reports" that were remarkable for their ideological confusion. Prudential, for instance, called its contributions program "part of a real attempt to integrate two different value systems: Those that are oriented toward making a living with those that are oriented toward making a life." Soulless corporations manned by automatons, beware. Equitable gave critics a blank check by stating that corporate existence is "a privilege subject to whatever requirements society decides to impose."[20]

The ideology supported by many corporate public relations departments also was evident in pronouncements by the Council on Foundations, supported primarily by large foundations and some 150 company contributors such as Exxon, Coca-Cola, and Time, Inc.[21] Financial support from business members has helped the Council to publicize its message that the corporate right to exist is "a grant from the public sector to the private sector, which confers upon the corporation a kind of trusteeship of the larger public good."[22] This suggests that corporations are political entities subservient to government, rather than economic organizations subject to market testing for efficient use of resources.

The era of "social responsibility" under consideration here culminated in creation of The President's Task Force on Private Sector Initiatives. Michael Deaver, then one of Ronald Reagan's three top assistants, was looking for a way to gain favorable White House publicity at a time when liberals were portraying Reagan tax and budget cuts as unfair to the poor. "We wanted a showcase," Deaver explained during my interview with him.[23] Deaver and his assistant James Rosebush, a former contributions office at Sohio, placed on the task force some of the most public relations-minded of corporate chairmen, including C. William Verity, Jr. of Armco, John Filer of Aetna Life & Casualty and Kenneth Dayton of Dayton-Hudson.

Along with allies such as John Gardner (Lyndon Johnson's Secretary of Health, Education and Welfare, and former chairman of Common Cause), these corporate leaders pushed through a recommendation that every company in the United States, large or small, give at least 2% of pretax net income to "nonprofit organizations engaged in public services." The 2% formula was not a new idea. Filer had chaired a privately sponsored commission that in 1975 had made the same recommendation. But this time, backers of "public–private partnership" were confident. Stanley Karman, director of the insurance industry's Center for Corporate Public Involvement, predicted that the Reagan task force might "finally break down conservative business resistance in this area." Lloyd Dennis, senior vice president at the First Interstate Bank of California, said "The juices are flowing. Public affairs heads are pushing the use of corporate resources in social areas. Their views are seeping up to chief executives."[24]

Some of the hopeful recipients of corporate largesse also were optimistic. Pablo Eisenberg, president of the Center for Community Change in Washington, explained that the task force "said once and for all that a Federal Government group has the major responsibility to twist elbows on corporate expenditures in this area, to go peer to peer and say we're going to judge our peers harshly if they don't move on this." John Gardner said, "Businessmen were not persuaded by the Filer Commission or by the 2% or 5% clubs, but now the recommendation is at a level they're more likely to listen to."[25]

In 1982 publicity concerning the task force recommendation led to a backlash of criticism. Some of it was public. Martin Anderson, who had recently resigned as top assistant to President Reagan for policy development, said that it was not "appropriate" for the government to tell corporations what their role should be. Robert Krieble, chairman of Loctite, said flatly, "I'm not interested in picking up welfare programs. I want to build self-reliance." Phil

Marcus, then director of the Institute of Educational Affairs, said that "Corporate officials are hedging their bets on 'Reaganomics' by demonstrating social sympathies with liberals in their giving programs."[26]

Michael Horowitz, then counsel to the director in the Office of Management and Budget, predicted that large national nonprofit organizations would be prime recipients of increased contributions. He saw enormous waste resulting:

> It's a largely unknown story, but the extent to which what we call "volunteer, nonprofit" organizations have become public service vendors, captured by professional staffs and lobbyists, is a terrible fact of life.[27]

Tom Pauken, director of ACTION, argued that "our responsibility as conservatives is to offer sensible alternatives to things which haven't worked, not just change one set of bureaucrats for another and say we've accomplished something just because they're off the Federal payroll."[28]

During 1982, more comments about reaffirming "bankrupt policies" were heard. Robert Woodson, president of the National Center for Neighborhood Enterprise, said,

> Just because some organizations may be fed by corporate rather than government dollars, that doesn't mean they'll be any more effective. Corporations won't be able to pick out the sheep from the goats. Even if they really want to, they're so overwhelmed with requests that all they can do is play it safe by going to the established, ineffective organizations.[29]

Senator David Durenberger (R-Minn.) said, "The big nonprofits fight like hell against any upstart that puts together a better service. It's built into any system—if somebody's got a relative corner of the market, they resist competition."[30]

Critics of the task force's embrace of contribution percentages and corporate social responsibility also argued that companies during the 1980s should not repeat the mistakes of the 1960s. A liberal professor, David Vogel of the University of California, noted that "Reagan's task force is doing the same thing LBJ did, trying to get corporations involved in a lot of activities beyond their area of competence." Conservative Allan Carlson of the Rockford Institute argued that "The private sector initiatives drive is a mirror image of the Great Society. It is run by many of the same people. Its advocates share the same presuppositions."[31]

Few heads of large corporations would speak out publicly against the 2% foot-in-the-door formula. Alexander Trowbridge, president of the National Association of Manufacturers, reported that some NAM members feared corporate critics would be drawing up good guy/bad guy lists based on the task force's recommendations. "It's very dangerous," the chief executive of a large Connecticut-based corporation said of the 2% quota. "It's ammo for the left, and we'll be shot." But many other CEOs dodged the issue.[32]

Often, they felt they had to. Some corporate leaders said privately they could not publicly attack federal government organs because they might soon be running to those subjects of criticism for special handouts. Following his departure from government, former Treasury Secretary William Simon summed up the result of a century of corporate public relations:

> During my tenure at Treasury I watched with incredulity as businessmen ran to the government in every crisis, whining for handouts or protection from the very competition that has made this system so productive. I saw Texas ranchers, hit by drought, demanding government-guaranteed loans; giant milk cooperatives lobbying for higher prices supports; major airlines fighting deregulation to preserve their monopoly status; giant companies like Lockheed seeking federal assistance to rescue them from sheer inefficiency; bankers, like David Rockefeller, demanding government bailouts to protect them from their ill-conceived investments; network executives, like William Paley of CBS, fighting to preserve regulatory restrictions and to block the emergence of competitive cable and pay TV. And always, such gentlemen proclaimed their devotion to free enterprise and their opposition to the arbitrary intervention into our economic life by the state. Except, of course, for their own case, which was always unique and which was justified by their immense concern for the public interest.[33]

In this sense, corporate contributions policy became subservient to government relations: Contributions officers sometimes were told to find out the favorite charities and activities of key regulators, and then offer support. The list of corporate contributors to Wolf Trap, favorite music and drama playground for the Washington elite, soared, even as some small and needy groups found their way still blocked, regardless of 2% formulas. As one corporate contributions officer said in 1983,

> There are some naive people who actually think that our contributions are contributions. They're not. They're public admissions of our fears—fear of a politician, fear of an executive at some other company, fear of the public interest groups . . .[34]

The cynicism of corporate "philanthropy" in the early 1980s was sometimes overwhelming. Building ties with governmental powers was their most important task, contributions officers often noted privately, but subtlety was important, so the field of corporate contributions was undergoing expansion. "My job is setting up the opportunities for us to innocently arrange deals," one manager explained:

I like to get our executives on the same charitable boards with the regulators, so they can build relationships in a third party atmosphere. It's worth a donation of $10,000 for us to have a neutral, innocuous place to meet. Another thing to notice is the amount of leverage you can get with corporate contributions.[35]

And yet, some 20 years after U.S. Steel's defeat brought home to corporate leaders the importance of corporate public relations subservience to governmental demands, the ambivalence was still evident. Corporate contribution percentages did not increase dramatically in 1982, despite task force recommendations, nor have they done so during the years since. The ideology of contributions continues to run up against real budgetary constraints, with the result that public relations personnel increasingly have to shuffle and mumble and apologize for not doing more.

Still, some amazing corporate grants are made. For instance, in 1984 Honeywell, Inc., made a grant of $125,000 to underwrite a 4-part series of seminars questioning arms spending. Honeywell had long been the target of "peace activists" who said they would continue demonstrating at the defense contractor's headquarters until Honeywell stopped military production. The seminars were an overture to the activists and were well-received, because to them it was proof that "Honeywell's top executives are responding to a massive civil disobedience campaign . . . " Once the series concluded, the campaign intensified, with several of the activists digging graves on Honeywell property to call attention to their opposition to weapon production, and others blocking Honeywell's entrance until police cars came.[36]

It was startling at times during 1985 to read the lists of corporate grant recipients: What purpose other than very short-term public relations appeasement was served by grants to the Center for Community Change, a politically-left organizing group, or to organizations that were suing companies on affirmative action grounds and arguing for "comparable worth"? The list of solid organizations favoring competitive enterprise that were frozen out in many contributions programs also is striking. As Charles Wohlstetter, chairman of Continental Telecom Inc., complained accurately, "corporate money is not invested in what polite radical-chic opinion considers 'unacceptable.' "[37]

During 1986, in governmental relations and contributions areas, as in others, the combat of collaborationist ideology and economic reality continued. The battle led to severe ethical dilemmas for corporate public relations managers. We will turn to some of those questions of ethics in the next chapter.

Ministers or Panderers: Issues Raised by the PRSA Code of Professional Standards, 1954–1986

The Public Relations Society of America (PRSA) was formed in 1948. One of its early presidents, Ed Lipscomb, gave a spiritual thrust to PRSA's role when he argued that "business still is looked upon for the most part as wholly secular – the pulpit as wholly spiritual," but "there is a group in America which is fully equipped and qualified to establish in this country a new level of leadership midway between pavement and pulpit . . . the public relations profession of America." Lipscomb said that PRSA members could "take the initiative in bringing about the integration of spiritual principles and material progress which, and which alone, can assure for us and our fellowmen a maximum of human happiness."[1]

Lipscomb had a messianic strain. When he spoke of public relations as a "great cause" and "consecrated service," some PRSA members guffawed. But others listened, and considered further action. Public relations men and women at that time generally were perceived as slick con artists. If they were ever to improve their reputation and become the secular ministers of Lipscomb's dream, they had to "get ethics." Some members may have had a genuine desire to heal their own occupation so that it could heal the world. Others, trained in presenting and promoting favorable images, saw the image-building usefulness of a PRSA code of ethics. Whatever the rationale, PRSA members went to work on a code and adopted the organization's official Code of Professional Standards in 1954.[2]

That code is still in effect with minor revisions (made in 1959, 1963, 1977, and 1983). "We pledge to conduct ourselves professionally, with truth, accuracy, fairness, and responsibility to the public," the Code declares, and then lists 14 articles adopted "to promote and maintain high standards of public service and ethical conduct among its members." Several of the articles are general in nature: "A member shall deal fairly with clients or employers . . . A member shall conduct his professional life in accord with the public interest . . . A member shall adhere to truth and accuracy and to generally accepted standard of good taste." Several are specific: "A member shall not encroach upon the professional employment of another member. Where there are two engagements, both must be assured that there is no conflict between them."[3]

Careful readers of the Code noted immediately a glittering lack of precision in the articles on what could be called "social responsibility." Adherence to "generally accepted standards of good taste" allowed many questionable practices to continue. Harvard University dean Paul Ylvisaker told one PRSA national convention:

> I read your Code of Professional Standards. I read it very carefully. And I compliment you . . . But I read one thing that scared the hell out of me. It says here: "A member has the affirmative duty of adhering to generally accepted standards of accuracy, truth and good taste." In other words, if you can document that the general standards are not so sharp, you're off the hook.[4]

PRSA members were off the hook again and again, but not when it came to financial arrangements. In 1962, eight years after adoption of the Code, PRSA's Grievance Board meted out the first PRSA penalty for code violation when it censured a member for trying to "steal" the account of another member. During the 1970s, only four cases of code violation were tried by PRSA "judicial panels," and only one penalty was incurred: suspension of membership for "flagrant account piracy." A reader of PRSA's code enforcement proceedings would conclude that only one of the then-10,000 PRSA members did anything wrong during that decade, and his sin was taking business from a fellow PRSA member.[5]

In the 1970s, therefore, it was clear that the Code of Professional Standards was partly a public relations device to allow claims of adherence to virtue, and partly a matter of constraining free competition. The former application was part of what philosopher Sissela Bok has noted: "Codes of ethics function all too often as shields . . ." The latter application became a concern to the Federal Trade Commission's Bureau of Competition, which threatened antitrust action against the PRSA unless the section banning "encroachment" upon another member's business was repealed. It was repealed, with even Frank Wylie, the 1978 PRSA president, admitting that "An ethic which protects the club-members is really no ethic at all."[6]

The phrase about adherence to "generally accepted standards" was retained. My interviewing in 1983 of 50 public relations practitioners at one of the ten largest U.S. corporations showed how that phrase was interpreted.

One top practitioner asked, "Does the word 'lie' actually mean anything anymore? In one sense, everyone lies, but in another sense, no one does, because no one knows what's true—it's whatever makes you look good." Another manager believed that the generally accepted standard was, "There is no such thing as truth. You judge actions depending on whether they're done by someone above you or someone below you. There's no right or wrong."[7]

Other public relations managers had their own definitions of Code-required adherence to truth and accuracy. One latter-day Pharisee espoused "fact accuracy" but "professional manipulation of impression." He insisted, "I don't lie. I've never lied. There's a fine line sometimes, but I've never had data in front of me and read off the wrong numbers to a reporter." The requirement for fair dealing with employers also was honored, but in curious ways. "You have to let [top executives] know you'll support them in whatever they do," one public relations manager said. "You'll lie for them, you'll cheat for them, you'll cover up for them," she stated, adding that "doing whatever it takes to get the job done" was "all in an honest day's work."[8]

In general, serious mention of the Code was a surefire sources of merriment among the practitioners interviewed. Words that make sense only if they have a clear and accepted objective definition—truth, public interest, and so on—were twisted like wax noses. One public relations manager called the Code a "farce." Another, more generous, simply termed it a "failure."[9] The Code did not even help the public relations of public relations. It appeared as one more indication of hypocrisy in an occupation scorned for promoting imagery rather than substance.[10] Codes of ethics were trendy during the late 1970s especially, but, as W. R. Inge put it, he who marries the spirit of an age soon finds himself a widower.[11]

Noting the problems of adherence to "social responsibility" and "generally accepted standards," some PRSA leaders over the years adopted a quasi-existentialist position based on advocacy of "individual responsibility." One former PRSA president, J. Carroll Bateman, often wrote that a virtuous public relations practitioner should "make his own appraisals and arrive at his own judgments," based on his own value systems. But a look at where such independent action has led us is not comforting. Public relations veterans know many tales of principled pain placated by paychecks.[12]

It was hard for "individual responsibility" to be effective when, as the title of one article on public relations in the 1980s contended, "There's No Shame Anymore." Writer Robert Kaus explained, "Washingtonians have been selling connections, or the appearance thereof ever since the town was a swamp, but until recently they always tried to be discreet about it." Not so the lobbyists of the new era, according to Kaus: "The crude atmosphere of quid pro quo" extended from the Capitol to the townhouse of a practitioner living on Capitol Hill who insisted that his residence made for key contacts because he had "children of congressmen coming over for slumber parties."[13]

In short, "responsibility to the public" was undefinable during the early 1980s, but trust in individual ethical judgment became problematic because there was no common sense of what such responsibility entailed. In his article Kaus noted that "until recently, there was something, less formal than a law, that at least held the corruption in check. This was a public morality and its disciplinary mechanism, shame." Public relations practitioners who stepped out of line had "fear of public embarrassment and scorn. This fear—and the secretiveness and hypocrisy that it entailed—served to limit the scope" of manipulative activities. This fear is gone.[14]

If Kaus was right and shame troubled few practitioners, an appeal to their senses of right and wrong was fruitless. An appeal of any sort, unless given tough enforcement, tended to be an exercise in hypocrisy, futility, or both. An effective public relations code would have had to include not only pious sentiments but painful penalties. If PRSA had been serious, it would have expelled members who "corrupt the channels of communication" (to quote one of the Code's clauses).[15] It would have provided models of what not to do by publicly explaining the reasons for expulsion, with names named. It would have brought shame into play. It did not.

The refusal to take ethics seriously was not because the subject was never brought up. As far back as 1957, Bateman was writing that basic goals of practitioners had to change if public relations was ever to win greater public acceptance. He noted that:

> To ourselves and to others we have too long—and perhaps wrongly—held ourselves out as 'molders of public opinion,' or to put it more bluntly, as professional persuaders. Persuasion is a means rather than an end.[16]

Bateman had criticized the tendency to "Sell the sizzle, not the steak," by asking:

> How long will it continue to work? Haven't we already perceived a deterioration of public confidence in communication that deals with sizzles instead of steaks? If those of us who are professionally engaged in the art of communication will not devise messages that inform and educate our audiences, are we not helping to degrade them?[17]

Following Bateman's initial attack, though, a run of defensiveness began. Writers in *Public Relations Journal* (*PRJ*) argued against "unrealistic pipe-dreams" which could "inhibit the objective reasoning necessary at this stage."[18] Questioning of ethics was called in *PRJ* "dreamy speculation" which could lead to an "orgy of self-examination."[19]

Throughout the 1960s, *PRJ* articles urged practitioners to dump any concern about "intangibles" and instead create a new, improved "image of smartness, Machiavellian smartness . . ."[20] One writer equated discussion of ethical questions with "contemplating our navels."[21] Questions of facticity or honesty seemed unimportant. Consultant Philip Lesly wrote, "In the arena of present 'attitude management,' not the facts but the *impression* people get of a situation is the real reality."[22] Public relations manager S. Ralph Dubrowin decried "disrespect for PR" and proclaimed that public relations counselors were experts in "Business Psychiatry."[23]

Along with praise for those who saluted the public relations flag came verbal harassment of those proposing alternatives. One PRSA leader, Dan Forrestal of Monsanto, insisted that "the temptation to be noble forever lurks in the hearts of men," but it had to go.[24] A *PRJ* editorial attacked critics of public relations ethics:

> Unless we can stand up and say, "I am proud to be in public relations," we are likely to lack confidence and may feel ashamed of ourselves and our field of work. In that event, we do not belong in the field and will do a kindness to all right-thinking public relations men and women if we enter upon another type of activity.[25]

During the 1970s, though, Watergate fallout led to new criticism of public relations by public relations managers, even within the trade magazine of the organization devoted to "PR for PR." Donald Danko complained that "many corporate communications programs are laden with half-truths."[26] Pierre Werka observed, "It would be comforting to believe that the barrier standing between us and better PR for PR is the fringe operator. But often the fringe operator is no more guilty of presenting a blurred picture than the upstanding, honorable practitioner."[27] Arthur Cuervo complained that since "mainstream practitioners engage in the engineering of consent . . . at the top of the PR enemies list should be the practitioners themselves."[28]

Once again, whenever the going got tough, cheerleading became common. Nineteenth-century practitioners such as Amos Kendall had been proud of turning down job offers from those with whom they had serious differences.[29] In the 1970s, though, rationalizations such as the following were typical:

> While the true professional should be willing to put his or her job on the line over ethical decision-making considerations, this is perhaps too ideological a position concerning reality. Indeed, if public relations people did terminate positions that forced them to compromise their ethical standards, managements and clients probably would have little difficulty replacing them with other communicators who had lower standards of morality.[30]

A PRSA report during 1981 acknowledged that the public relations field was "now confronted with critical questioning. Its practitioners are questioning its status and role as pointedly as outsiders." It suggested use of a new vocabulary to make public relations actions "appear" more ethical. For instance, public relations men and women were told that they should not talk about plans to "master the publics," but should instead emphasize their desire "to achieve mutual adaptations."[31]

Public Relations Journal in 1985 trumpeted the beginning of a bimonthly column on ethics. In editor Michael Winkleman's words,

> PRJ's ethics columns will seek not so much to provide guidance as to wrestle with demons . . . We're expecting our readers to contribute their own vignettes, their tales of ethical dilemmas and long sessions of doubt, questioning, and even remorse.[33]

The initial ethics column, in February, 1985, was simply a series of generalizations by PRSA official Donald McCammond about "heightened awareness of ethical imperatives." The supposed good news was that "discussion and debate on the topic of ethics at conferences, luncheon conversations, and even cocktail parties seems to have increased."[33] But editor Winkleman insisted that change would come:

> Soul-searching, hard-hitting, and controversial are some of the key words that guide our editorial meeting these days . . . Look for more issues and controversy, more dilemmas and problems, more soul-searching and hard-hitting, thought-provoking writing in these pages as the months go on.[34]

The second ethics column, in April, 1985, reported public relations professor Donald K. Wright's irritation when a banquet speaker vociferously attacked public relations: "Here he was expressing public ridicule and exhibiting professional prejudice against public relations. At least a dozen public relations people sat there, listened, and never even objected to these remarks."[35]

Wright then reported on his research into public relations ethics:

> We borrowed questionnaires and methodologies from social psychologists in order to learn more about the basic moral and ethical perceptions of people in our field. These studies rank the severity of judgment on 50 activities ranging from killing, robbery, and arson, to making huge profits, charging too much interest, lying, cheating, and failing to keep promises."[36]

Wright observed that "over the years, as our Western society has become more reformed [sic] and liberal, all of our value systems have become more permissive." Because public relations practitioners answered Wright's questionnaire in much the same way others did, he concluded that "Scientific evidence now exists to show we're as decent, moral, and ethical as the rest of our society—not that we didn't know it anyway."[37]

The June column, by a newspaper-editor-turned-public-relations-manager, compared an ethical dilemma he had faced as an editor with one he had faced in public relations, and reported that the public relations outcome was more ethical.[38]

According to editor Winkelman's plan, there should have been another of the bimonthly columns in August, but there was not. Nor was there a column in the September, October, November, or December issues. A column did appear in January, 1986. It suggested that "Public relations relates to enhancing perceptions of trust," so "Let's be honest with each other."[39] After that outburst, the ethics column disappeared once more.

One of Bateman's pessimistic comments in 1973 might seem like an appropriate way to end this chapter: He felt as if he "was on a huge merry-go-round in time, that he had heard it all before . . . and that in reality no genuine progress had been made in the public relations profession over the years."[40]

But there is hope, if public relations managers and others understand the wisdom behind Judge Learned Hand's view that public relations as practiced in his time was "a black art," but one that had "come to stay. Every year adds to the potency, to the finality of its judgments." Learned Hand made that suggestion because he observed the tendency to rely on public relations when an organization's future is in the hands of an abstract "public opinion," with governmental edict as the enforcing arm. He knew that as the stakes rise, or are perceived to rise, the pressure to deceive increases. Because that is the case, studies indicating lack of public relations effectiveness lead to the conclusion that, somehow, more effective manipulations must be devised.[41]

Many of the academically-prevalent "social responsibility" arguments even increase the push to deception, rather than ameliorate it. If organizations are supposed to serve a liberally-defined "public interest" rather than the private interests of owners, then there will be additional pressure to allow the newly-declared de facto commanders of the corporation – the "public" – a complete look at the books.

Clearly, however, a private corporation cannot operate with all its plans publicly debated and all of its competitive strategies public. There is discrepancy between public demands for access and what private managers actually can allow. The gap between a professed ideal of public access and the reality of private secrets is inevitably filled by the smiling public relations staffer. His job is to indicate that all important items are being made public, when of course they are not.

If public relations is not to be "a black art," one goal of those in the field must be to reassert the distinction between public and private relations. The lost art of saying with a smile, "None of your business," should be reintroduced. When public relations men and women deceive to avoid disclosing information which is truly not the public's business, there is one alternative that does not bring added disgrace: They must straightforwardly state that private is not public.

The pressure now is enormous to go the other way, toward more apparent disclosure. This pressure comes not only from governmental bodies yearning for more power, but from companies attempting to use regulations for competitive advantage. When a manager witnesses constant lobbying to write obscure but crucial provisions into tax legislation, and constant financial flumgoggery to pull millions of dollars through the loopholes developed by the lobbyists, how then will he sort out legitimately private conduct from that which is not?

Truly free enterprise is based on "market discipline," which means the opportunity to lose as well as to win. If the federal government provides not the opportunity to pursue happiness but the guarantee of obtaining it, does not everything become the public's business? Institutional problems do not cause illegitimate actions by individuals, but yet, when the stakes are so high, how many public relations managers might be expected to honor PRSA's code?

Establishment of a workable Code will require, among other things, a lowering of the stakes. If the possible ends (such as corporate dissolution at governmental hands) were not so disastrous, then the pressure to use extraordinary means would not be as great. Improvement in ethical standards will require, among other changes, a re-examination of the public–private divide and a struggle for the reemergence of private relations. The next chapter will put the current ethics questions in context by discussing those other needed changes and then returning to questions of individual responsibility.

CHAPTER FOURTEEN

The Four-Fold Discipline

Almost every major public relations textbook of the early and mid-1980s contended or implied that the problems of public relations are at the periphery of the occupation. Were it not for a few corrupt practitioners, for fly-by-nighters who falsely use the title "public relations counsel," or for certain mildly troublesome practices, public relations would be clothed in such magnificent robes that even insouciant children would not be able to detect nakedness triumphant.[1]

Some textbook authors complained about those who "usurp the title" of public relations practitioners; for instance, the Chicago prostitute arrested for soliciting after she had passed out business cards with her name, phone number, address, and the two words, "Public Relations." But authors avoided key trouble spots. For instance, Fraser Seitel, director of public affairs at Chase Manhattan Bank and author of *The Practice of Public Relations*, minimized the problems at large institutions, then complained that, "There is nothing to prevent someone with little or no formal training from 'hanging out a shingle' as a public relations specialist. Such frauds embarrass professionals in the field."[2] Lawrence Nolte, in *Fundamentals of Public Relations*, noted that some "use the designation as a respectable cover for activities which are not public relations at all."[3]

Blaming the periphery, though, does not come to grips with the central problems of public relations. Nor does it explain why public relations progress over the past 30 years has been so small that the apologies offered now are virtual repetitions of those made then.

To see that history does not repeat itself but excuses do, it's worth looking at a short book written by J. A. R. Pimlott in 1951, *Public Relations and American Democracy*. Practitioners then, according to Pimlott, argued that:

> Their indifferent reputation is due to the incompetence and dishonesty of a minority of their number – to "the lunatic fringe of the profession, the headline wheedlers, the something-for-nothing boys," to "the antics of the quacks and charlatans who cling to the fringe of our profession," to "the snide, weasel-minded, smart, conscienceless lads."[14]

Pimlott agreed that:

> There is something in the argument. As an explanation of the persistently poor reputation of the group it is, however, neither probable nor in accordance with the facts. Other professions carry lunatic and even dishonorable fringes without suffering much loss of esteem; and the truth is that public distrust arises less from tyros and quacks on the fringe than from the more widely publicized activities of some of the leading figures.[5]

A third of a century after Pimlott's book, attacks on "the fringe" continue. This book, though, has focused on the center: Railroads, utilities, steel companies, and so on. It has shown that the problem is in the nature of modern public relations ideology itself, with its emphasis on collaborationism, its low regard for truly private enterprise, its Bernaysian desire to manipulate in the public interest of avoiding chaos.

A program to improve public relations, therefore, must concentrate not on the periphery, but on the center. What follows is a long-range, 4-part program to do just that. The program would require changes in thinking about government, the role of corporate management, public relations education, and public relations ethics. It could be called a four-fold discipline because it would require a new discipline in four spheres of thought and action, rather than a grasping for immediate benefit.

GOVERNMENT

William Leggett was an editorial writer on the New York *Evening Post* during the 1830s. Advocates of government control over the economy were arguing even then, according to Leggett, "that because our government has been instituted for the benefit of the people, it must therefore have the power to do whatever may seem to conduce to the public good."[6] But Leggett objected:

> Under the sanction of such a principle, a government can do any thing on pretense of acting for the public good. It will become the mere creature of designing

politicians, interested speculators, or crack-brained enthusiasts. It will gradually concentrate to itself all the reserved rights of the people; it will become the great arbiter of individual prosperity; and thus, before we know it, we shall become the victims of a new species of despotism.[7]

According to Leggett, governmental regulation generally "reduces men from a dependence on their own exertions, to a dependence on the caprices of their Government." A regulatory authority has the power "of directing its patronage first here and then there; of bestowing one day and taking back the next . . ." The result is "a disguised despotism," with government as "the capricious dispenser of good and evil."[8]

Leggett noted, at a time when government's economic role was still small, that "by frequent exercises of partial legislation, almost every man's personal interests have become deeply involved in the result of the contest." That was good observation, but not particularly prophetic. Leggett's prescience emerged when he described the long-term dangers of legislation and regulation benefiting special interests:

One of the greatest supports of an erroneous system of legislation, is the very evil it produces. When it is proposed to remedy the mischief by adopting a new system, every abuse which has been the result of the old one becomes an obstacle to reformation. Every political change, however salutary, must be injurious to the interests of some, and it will be found that those who profit by abuses are always more clamorous for their continuance than those who are only opposing them from motives of justice or patriotism, are for their abandonment.[9]

A self-perpetuating system of that sort is, by definition, unstoppable. And yet, in the United States during the 1980s, there have been strong attempts to stop it by developing new restraints on governmental aggrandizement. It is too early to tell whether the new discipline will take hold, but more Americans seem to be realizing the wisdom in Leggett's belief that:

Governments have no right to interfere with the pursuits of individuals, as guaranteed by those general laws, by offering encouragements and granting privileges to any particular class of industry, or any select bodies of men, inasmuch as all classes of industry and all men are equally important to the general welfare, and equally entitled to protection.[10]

At the same time, however, there are still strong proponents of public-private partnership, which inevitably involves the granting of privilege to a particular class of industry, and of "new industrial policy," which represents the direct offering of encouragements to particular industries and firms. As long as such sugar plums are there for the gulping, many corporate leaders will feel an obligation to grab for them, despite the long-term costs of such behav-

ior. Thus, part one of the four-fold discipline requires a vast political movement in this country toward the Leggett principle that "Governments possess
no delegated right to tamper with individual industry a single hair's-breadth
beyond what is essential to protect the rights of person and property."[11]

CORPORATE MANAGEMENT

In 1985 many large American corporations had over 100 persons on their central public relations staffs. One company with $15 billion in sales had a staff of
five. That was possible only because of the political philosophies of the top executives at that company, which will be referred to as Company Q.[12]

For instance, at most companies media relations experts do exactly what
the "evolution" of public relations suggests they should do. They cooperate
fully with reporters, set up interviews with executives and managers, suggest
favorable stories, provide "perspective" on unfavorable developments, and so
on.

At Company Q, the general rule is, "Don't talk with the press, don't set up
interviews." The logic goes: Why do reporters ask questions? To gain information. If we have substantive information that we have worked hard to gain
and that may be useful in our business decision-making, why give it away? If
we have nonsubstantive information, why waste our time, the reporter's time
and the readers' time, with fluff? Others can worry about image-building; we
want to create better products.

At most large companies, a highly-trained contributions staff attempts to
determine how best to exercise "social responsibility" by making grants to
worthwhile organizations. Difficult decisions about relative worthiness are
made easier by the dispatching of grants to charities favored by back-
scratching executives and tax-writing congressmen, but that is all part of the
challenge.

At Company Q, the contributions policy is simple: No trading of favors.
Company executives are not encouraged to join nonprofit boards. The CEO
does not ask his counterparts at other companies to support his favorite
charities. No public interest contributions. A part-time staffer simply sees
which nonprofit institutions employees use and value the most, and provides
support to those institutions commensurate with employee use. For instance,
if employees make use of a community nonprofit hospital, the company will
contribute to that hospital.

At most large companies, governmental relations experts develop complex
attempts to have favorable clauses inserted into tax and protectionist legislation. Company lobbyists keep busy attending $500-a-person receptions and
$1,000-a-plate dinners. Former key congressional staffers are hired to lobby
their friends still on the job.

At Company Q, a simple, principled policy is followed: Do not lobby for particular advantage. Because executives believe that taxes generally are too high and federal regulations too numerous, Company Q's position is to favor at all times lower taxes and less regulation. A part-time Washington governmental affairs representative explains that position in special situations when defensive lobbying may be essential due to efforts of other companies.

We could look at the differences between the policies of most large companies and Company Q in many other public relations areas, but the point should be clear. Here are two entirely different ways of conducting public relations business. The style of most companies is the culmination of public relations "evolution." The Company Q style may be an endangered species, and is almost entirely ignored within many public relations classrooms.

When asked why the Company Q style is not presented as a real alternative, the typical answer is that such a public relations policy is clearly unrealistic: It may have worked in a simpler society, but it cannot work now. Some even suggest that public relations experience over the past century has proven that typical procedures work better than Q-style.

In a limited sense, the question of realism can be dealt with quickly, by examining whether Company Q has suffered serious public relations blows, as our common theory would expect. Some results are in: A reporter cajoled by other companies missed his favored treatment and may have given Company Q fewer polite press mentions than it could otherwise have accumulated. It seems likely that some tax breaks perhaps achievable by fervent lobbying have not been seized. Some grant-receiving groups pampered at other companies have muttered about the social irresponsibility of Company Q. And yet, Company Q's media relations are generally positive because reporters know the company is not playing games with them. When Company Q does lobby to prevent ravishment at the hands of its aggressively-lobbying competitors, politicians listen, perhaps because of a grudging respect for rare commodities such as political principle, which they do not regularly see around themselves or even in the mirror. Community organizations that actually serve Company Q's employees make sure that any complaints from employees receive prompt response.

It is very difficult to measure the pluses and minuses of Company Q's public relations policy, because we are not in a laboratory situation. It can be said, though, that Company Q has not been blown out of the water; it has had substantial savings in public relations personnel costs and expenses with no demonstrable disasters; Company Q policy is not demonstrably unrealistic. Nor has the common public relations method been proven successful. As this book shows, public relations managers often have been strange dentists making as many cavities as they fill.

Other large companies, then, could adopt Q-style public relations, if they wanted to. Movement in that direction would take considerable executive bravery, because it is easier to conform. But if a CEO is tired of a public relations department that is both unethical and ineffective, if he wants to spend less money on propaganda and more on improving and marketing products, and if he is willing to take some heat in order to reestablish private relations, he can make a difference. Discipline would be necessary because there would be some short-run costs, but benefits would come eventually.

The second part of this four-fold discipline – an executive willingness to take risks – would become less significant if a vast political movement were to establish Leggett's principles of minimal government. Given the likelihood of *some* movement in that direction but not a sweeping change, initiative among top executives becomes crucial.

PUBLIC RELATIONS EDUCATION

For many years professors of economics had a problem in their teaching. They could explain to students how companies in the widget business should price their product. They could equip students to maximize return for their firms, all other things being equal. But if the bottom fell out of the market for reasons unconnected to individual product quality, or if the government rapidly expanded money supply and threw off all previous calculations, then the students were stuck. They were learning what we now call microeconomics, but they had not been exposed to the bigger picture.

Concentration on microeconomics also limited student research possibilities. Thesis or paper writers were asked to analyze the immediate effects of a given policy, or its effects only on a special group. Their microeconomic analysis was unable to examine the long-run effects of a policy not only on a special group but on all groups. Secondary consequences were overlooked.

Eventually, though, the subdiscipline of macroeconomics came into being. Macroeconomics professors looked not merely at the immediate but at the longer-run effects of any action. Useful analysis of this kind traced the consequences of a policy not merely for one group but for many. Students were taught the interrelationship of Washington, Wall Street, and Main Street.

Public relations education is now where economics education used to be. The culminating course of a typical undergraduate sequence is a campaigns course, often coupled with an internship. Students learn how to coordinate public relations activities to produce an effect beneficial to their real or imagined client. This is useful and important training. But where do students learn to examine the impact of particular activities on the overall political, social, and economic climate? Or, perhaps more immediately relevant where do they learn how the overall climate may affect the success of their particular campaign?

This last question is not merely one for theoretical contemplation. Irving Kristol has observed that, "One of the reasons the large corporations find it so difficult to persuade the public of anything is that the public always suspects them of engaging in clever public relations instead of simply telling the truth."[13] Practitioners at small companies as well as large, regardless of their personal integrity, tend to be considered guilty by association with a scorned public relations occupation. Reporters such as Isadore Barmash of The New York Times point to public relations and complain that "much of our life today represents the reaction to manipulated behavior, to words and deeds of delusion, all of which leads to actions that are the result of deception."[14]

When reporters such as Barmash are busy blaming public relations practitioners for an "abuse of truth and reality," how receptive will they be to the next press release received, no matter how skillful its composition? If students do not learn that their work's success or failure is related to public attitudes toward public relations generally, then they will be like the microeconomists, unable to adjust their own efforts as societal conditions change.

In one sense the above paragraph is obvious, but the obvious does not seem to have sunk in. For instance, a recent public relations textbook noted that, "The events at Three Mile Island did not reflect well on public relations practitioners," but a "bright spot" was "the boon Three Mile Island provided to public relations," because more practitioners were employed in an attempt to pick up the pieces.[15] That is like cheering broken windows because they temporarily create full employment among glaziers.

To make public relations students aware of the long-term detriments that might result even from short-term successes, public relations professors should begin teaching courses in what could be called macro public relations. The distinction between micro and macro public relations would be similar in many ways to the traditional micro–macro divide in economics. For instance, microeconomists analyze the output of a single firm operating within the constraints of its market, while macroeconomists analyze the level of output for the whole economy. Similarly, micro public relations tells students how to do public relations work within a particular organization; macro public relations teaches them to analyze the impact of large public relations campaigns on American society or significant parts of it.

Macro public relations courses would have a strong ethics component, but they would not be proclaiming theoretical ethics in a vacuum. Courses taking into account the dimensions of politics and corporate management discussed above would be able to delve realistically into questions such as:

• The most frequent excuse for deception given by public relations practitioners, that "our lies counterbalance the lies of others." Sissela Bok, in her book Lying, noted that such claims are extraordinarily prone to misinterpretation and bias:

Even if it were right to reciprocate in this way, it is often hard to know when others are lying. Even those who want to return the deception they encounter are bound to make mistakes. If we feel free to deceive those we suspect of having lied, we are likely to invite vast increases in actual deception . . ."[16]

The supply curve of lies pushes up the demand curve, and vice versa.

• The ethics and consequences of viewing questions of public information in adversary terms. As Bok observed, "All too often, the lie directed at adversaries is a lie to friends as well." Even lies invoking self-defense, or organizational defense, tend to backfire, since "self defense lies can permeate all one does, so that life itself turns into 'living a lie.' "[17]

• The effect of public relations manipulation on public relations men and women themselves. Practitioners interviewed in one study contended that the road to public relations success lies through manipulation of public opinion—for the public good, of course, and only to counteract the negative publicity which enemies have provided. But Bok noted the repercussions of such practice: Those "involved in collective practices of deceit give up all ordinary assumptions about their own honesty and that of others."[18]

• The claim of harmlessness. Bok observed that even small distortions have an effect, for "Lies tend to spread. Disagreeable facts come to be sugarcoated."[19] Even the apparently trivial has a cumulative impact, for acceptance of small lies leads to acceptance of large lies, and those who have been lied to in large ways tend to consider lying to others the only way to travel, in a natural reaction to disappointment.

• The effect of "manipulating public opinion" on American society generally. Political movements of the 1970s (which have continued into the 1980s) show, in Bok's words, that:

Millions of the lied-to are now resentful, disappointed, and suspicious. They feel wronged; they are wary of new overtures. And they look back on their past beliefs and actions in the new light of the discovered lies. They see that they were manipulated, that the deceit made them unable to make choices for themselves according to the most adequate information available, unable to act as they would have wanted to act had they known all along."[20]

It might be argued that students are not ready to understand some negative aspects of public relations, and that they will find out what goes on soon enough without the danger of premature discouragement. There is often an emphasis on teaching use of the tools of the trade, without mention of how those tools should be used. But should students be asked to give up the goal of getting a good education, which requires development and use of critical faculties, just because they are desirous of getting a good job? As the historian Henry Adams wrote about his nineteenth-century education, "Winter and summer were hostile, and the man who pretended they were not was . . . a schoolmaster—that is, a man employed to tell lies to little boys."[21]

Again, this third part of the four-fold discipline cannot stand alone. It will require movements along the governmental and corporate management tracks: The more movement there, the less pressure here. But, under any likely scenario, a new type of public relations teaching will be needed, one that provides long-run education and not just short-term job placement.

PUBLIC RELATIONS ETHICS

After working in a major corporate public relations department for four years during the 1950s, Alan Harrington wrote *Life in the Crystal Palace*, published by Knopf in 1959. In it Harrington examined one foundation of the Bernays approach: "At the base of the public relations man's craft is the assumption that he can manipulate the thoughts of others—in short, that people are (in relation to him) stupid. If they weren't, after all, he couldn't exist."[22]

Harrington also pointed out that there was not much concern about lying among his former colleagues, because it appears that the word hardly had any meaning within their solipsistic world views:

> A reputable PR practitioner never deliberately lies. Rather he sees before him a world of mobile and malleable truths. A ball of wax is a ball of wax . . . In the world of public relations, facts can be shaped with no damage to anyone's conscience.[23]

Harrington's definition of public relations practice thus became, logically, "the craft of arranging the truth so that people will like you. Public relations specialists make flower arrangements of the facts, placing them so that the wilted and less attractive petals are hidden by sturdy blooms." The goal is "to select and distort the facts in such a way that our clients will appear before the public in a good light. This could, severely, be called the art, science, skill, dodge, or trade of lying." The only sense is which this bothered his former colleagues, Harrington observed sarcastically, was that most were " 'educated' people with dim or corroded memories of classic principles—which they can always summon up when they need them from Bartlett's."[24]

Three decades after Harrington wrote, the objective of stating "the truth" is in even lower regard. Bartlett's quotation books are still brought off the shelves for speechwriting, but belief about the malleability of truth may even have been replaced by a quasi-Marxist notion that there are two kinds of truth—"our" truth and "their" truth, as experts in dialectics say. In many large public relations organizations, "our" truth produces social cohesion, and "their" truth is whatever opposes an ever-changing public relations line, and is what will lead to chaos unless resolutely beaten back.

My interviews of public relations practitioners in 1983 brought out some of the "ball of wax" thinking described by Harrington. One media relations manager explained that he was constantly attempting to assess what he could get away with:

> You end up trying out lines on reporters, ready to retreat if they challenge us, but they accept them most of the time. Remember, what they're trying to do is to tear us down so the guys at the bar will hoot and holler, but we're trying to build something, and we're not going to let them get in our way.[25]

Many corporate issue analysis managers explicitly suggested that there is no such thing as objective truth: Information is subjective, and to be used as weaponry. "Our truth is as good as our opponents' truth," one said. Another issue analyst explained that:

> We decide which position we want to push, then we hire some "objective" experts to write the papers which will become the official basis for our decision. For instance, the new industrial policy debate wasn't shaping up in our favor. It was important to refocus attention away from electronics, so for a couple of thousand dollars each for the right professors we could buy the _____ name and get not only a lot more attention, but credit for making a thorough appraisal of the subject.[26]

All the world is a John le Carre novel, with "legends" constantly in the making and counter-plots urged as the only defense against plotting; as one "issues manager" explained, "Someone puts out polls, you put out counter-polls. Someone hires academics, you hire other academics."[27]

The fourth discipline necessary to make public relations once again serve private enterprise and not savage it, then, is an establishment of basic honesty as an essential principle of dealing with each other. Private enterprise is founded on the inviolability of contract, contract backed up in the extreme by courts but in everyday behavior, when the system is working, by trust. Trust cannot survive when everything is seen as a ball of wax which can be retwisted to illegitimate advantage day by day.

The four-fold discipline, then, is crucial. Instead of looking for favors from government, we have to recreate a system of political economy in which we depend on our own hard work. Instead of using public relations to grease the easy slide of Washington, corporate executives must be willing to suffer the consequences if some short-term boons are sacrificed for the long-term benefits of reinstituting private relations. Instead of educating students to fit in, professors should teach their graduates to stand out. Instead of assuming that all is relative, public relations managers need to grapple—both for personal and societal salvation—with the idea of the existence of objective truth.

A Word to
Corporate Executives

It would be wonderful to conclude this book by suggesting that a public relations upheaval is imminent – but that would be wishful thinking. Some signs of discomfort are apparent, yet paychecks placate the pained, and a lack of perceived alternatives creates caution.

Some public relations managers even seem to function on the principle of "the worse, the better," with disasters leading to an expansion of job opportunities. As noted, Three Mile Island was seen as a boon to public relations.[1] (In a similar way, the Chernobyl disaster may have contributed to an expansion of opportunities for Soviet public relations officials.) The wages of deception appeared bountiful to those without full knowledge of the consequences.

So it has to be said here that many corporate public relations managers, judging from their trade magazines and comments, have three major goals as we head toward the 1990s.

First, if we take them at their word, they want to do some good for their companies. They know that the boom of the 1980s hasn't made big business much more popular than it was during the floundering 1970s. Logic and evidence to the contrary, new calls for socialism are only a recession away.

Second, public relations managers want to refurbish the image of public relations. The Rodney Dangerfields of corporate life grow justifiably sad when both corporate CEOs and neighborhood barflys call them names. In public opinion polls about occupations, public relations men and women beat out used car sellers, but there is little satisfaction in that.[2]

Third, many public relations managers want what many other corporate managers want: More authority, bigger budgets, larger staffs, and so on. Public relations workers, however, cannot develop and market high-flying products. Like those in other staff departments, their rank depends on how useful they are — or how useful they make themselves appear.

Those three goals are not new, nor are they unhealthy for business when taken in the order given above: Help your company, help your occupation, help yourself. When the order is reversed, though, we have managers acting in ways that glorify themselves but harm their organizations. That's the situation in much of corporate public relations today. That's the problem faced by corporate CEOs who want to take charge of their public relations departments and turn them into useful adjuncts rather than trojan horses.

A number of leading public relations executives today were frustrated public relations managers two decades ago. If their companies had remained aloof from the tendency to take on a higher profile, they would have been like small-town dentists called on to fix occasional cavities: Keep that item out of the press, put out a press release on our plant closing, and so on. They could call themselves Painless Parkers and give away balloons and lollypops, but essentially they had minor and unpopular, yet necessary, jobs.

The Public Relations Society of America's magazine in 1972 pointed out an alternative: "Increasing corporate concern and commitment in the social area is giving corporate PR people a much stronger story to communicate. But more importantly, it is providing PR professionals with new opportunity for highest-level involvement and responsibility . . . There is going to be a big brass ring up for grabs in many American companies in the next decade."[3]

The phrase "more importantly" was crucial. The history of corporate public relations has been dominated by the grab for big brass rings. Instead of trying to communicate information that folks outside companies need to know, many public relations workers have seen their role as one of furthering corporate activities in nonbusiness areas. To that end, as this book has shown, many have embraced an ideology opposed to private enterprise.

According to that ideology, corporations are to be managed not in the interest of stockholders and employees, but in "the public interest." Who, though, defines the public interest? If companies live by opinion polling during this age of philosophical confusion, then public relations becomes merely the tail of a potentially rabid dog. If companies bow to politicians or media stars, the door is open for demagoguery and the arrogance of self-professed messiahs.

According to the new public relations ideology, the public has a right to know intimate details of corporate finance and production; that makes sense if companies are portrayed as public servants. Who, though, defines the limits? Public relations managers who have been proclaiming the importance of answering reporters' questions find it hard to say, "None of your business."

According to the new public relations ideology, a substantial chunk of corporate profits must be contributed to various causes designated as worthy. But how much is enough, and who should do the choosing? Already there are vocal demands that 5% or 10% of profits be turned over to "community" foundations. The more corporations do, the more they are asked to do. They can never do enough, once the company treasury is seen as common grazing land.

The new ideology *has* heightened the importance of corporate public relations. But is has also led to new scorn for public relations and its practitioners, both inside and outside companies.

Farsighted corporate executives know that information about a company's internal operations, in a private enterprise economy, must be the company's business. So they resent public relations activities, and wonder why they are paying big salaries for "boundary-spanners" who cannot be entirely trusted. Sooner or later, they tell their public relations managers to hunker down.

Astute reporters see that public relations managers, caught between an ideology of "openness" and a command to protect company secrets, are speaking out of both sides of their mouths. Instead of giving accurate comments or a straight "no comment," many public relations men and women try to sidestep questions and manipulate the press. Reporters who see this like the new style even less than when they were shut out entirely; now, their time is being wasted.

Public relations managers who are self-aware see that they are being trapped in a corner. Boundary-spanning hubris has left them still removed from the public, but often not part of business either. In the middle ground they have been unsuccessful as spokesman for anyone, but have merely sown confusion about the purpose of corporations.

Ultimately, questions of corporate and social organization do come down to questions of purpose. Issues of the relationship of community and individual, or public and private, go far beyond public relations and the issues that can be covered succinctly in this specialized book. Given the philosophical, social, and cultural challenge of modernity, there is tremendous demand for what Bernays called "human gods," or at least big brothers, to make things work. To their credit, some public relations prophets of government-business collaboration have tried to unite through their activities public purpose and private profit, client goals and cultural needs. But their striving has been losing, because they have taken the turn toward centralization of power rather than decentralization and freedom.

Because this book began with a look at thoughts of private-relations thinking during the late 18th- and early 19th-centuries, we will return for one quick peek. Most of the founders two centuries ago opposed those who said that "public" goals should have primacy over private interests. They argued that progress was most likely to occur when private interests were pursued without obstacle. Knowing man's desire to seize power under the cloak of public spirit-edness, they saw that liberty was possible when counterbalancing forces checked each other from becoming too powerful, and therefore allowed groups of individuals to pursue their own interests.

When Alexis de Tocqueville visited America during the 1830s, he was impressed that the United States had so many different sectors of the political economy. Governmental hegemony was not much of a threat because a number of vital social institutions—education, aid to the poor, and so forth—were in the hands of community groups. These groups were more responsive to their constituencies than the European bureaucracies of de Tocqueville's time tended to be.

The unmistakable trend in the American social system during at least the past 50 years, however, has been toward a society dominated by two sectors, one corporate and the other governmental. The two sectors have taken on much of the work of society, with community organizations and individuals often relegated to the back of the bus. Americans have fallen into the habit of sitting back and hoping that the problems of society will be taken care of by one superpower sector or the other.

First came government's turn, but in recent years government has been seen by the American people to possess not just the bulk of a rhinoceros but the brain as well. The result of such disenchantment is that Americans are asking businesses to take care of social problems that government has handled ineffectively. Public relations managers have been eager to grab the big brass ring without often enough asking the basic question: Are corporations being asked to do what they cannot do economically and do not have a right to do morally?

The economic limits ought to be clear, although they seem to be ignored with amazing frequency. A little simple arithmetic will show that even enthusiastic corporations can exercise "social consciousness" that will be external to direct company interests only to a limited degree. Businesses are rightfully called on to improve products, productivity, and working conditions. They need a certain level of profits to use for new capital expenditures and to stay competitive in the investment market generally. When those obligations are met, throwing the money that remains at a large social problem external to the corporation will hardly scratch the surface. (I once calculated that the Du Pont Company's total annual dividends would keep the Department of Health and Human Services running for less than half a day.)

Corporate executives should not take refuge in economic arguments alone, however; for advocates of "social responsibility" may then engage in a "salami strategy" of requesting one small slice after another: Why not fund the art exhibit? Why not take over management of a faltering school program? The expense of individual activities at the margin is not that great. Rather than just talking dollars and cents, executives should insist that, as a matter of principle, corporate power in nonmarket spheres should be strictly limited. For if every business could somehow escape the discipline of the market system to take on a variety of social tasks, the obvious question for business leaders would be: By what right have you, as citizens with stewardship for particular economic concerns, assumed these additional powers?

The two most common definitions of democracy, after all, are: (a) operating through direct elections, and (b) giving people what they want (in the case of business, as seen through the market mechanism). Business has democratic legitimacy only when it is controlled by the market and does what the market wants it to do. It is not hard to predict the criticism that would develop if corporations followed the more radical "social responsibility" arguments and started using their power to run, and eventually control, everything from social welfare programs to anticrime campaigns.

For both economic and ethical reasons, then, corporations should not be relied on to remove social chestnuts from the fire. In the long run, the effective programs are those generated, organized, and funded by the individuals and community groups most affected by problems, not by outsiders, however well-meaning. Similarly, corporate responsibility does begin at home, in the way an organization treats the people who are directly and most seriously affected by its activities. If, for instance, a company's relationships with employees are flawed, no amount of papering over (by an extra gift to a local charity or by Thanksgiving turkeys to the faithful) will be acceptable as excuse or ploy.

In short, if we understand Constitutional political theory, we should begin emphasizing private relations rather than public relations. A corporation should try to make its own operations "a city on a hill," and should encourage other groups to do likewise with their own operations. Corporations should be unashamed about staking out large areas of private relations and consistently maintaining their perogatives. With courtesy but firmness, public relations managers should learn to tell overly-demanding fundraisers, reporters, or politicians, "None of your business."

This will cause resentment at first. But, if corporate initiatives are accompanied by changes in other areas, as discussed in the previous chapter, the other shoe will drop. In the limited areas that are legitimately public business, public relations managers will be able to be forthright. Reporters will find out that they are being told the truth. Both corporate reputations and the image of public relations will improve.

Some public relations managers who have grabbed the big brass ring during the past decade, though, will not want to go back to being small-town dentists. Real change will come only if top corporate executives decide to push for a revamping of their public relations programs, over the objections of some of their current managers. If those executives work at thinking through the relationship of private enterprise and public relations, they will be on solid theoretical ground. If they rethink their own operations they will be on solid practical ground. There is no better time to start than during the early years of the Constitution's third century.

NOTES

INTRODUCTION
Asking Basic Questions

1. Joseph McKerns, "The Limits of Progressive Journalism History," *Journalism History*, Autumn, 1977, p. 88.

2. Kenneth Henry, *Defenders and Shapers of the Corporate Image* (New Haven: College and University Press, 1972), pp. 89–90.

3. Peter M. Sandman, David M. Rubin, & David B. Sachsman, *Media: An Introductory Analysis of American Mass Communications* (Englewood Cliffs, N.J.: Prentice-Hall, 1976), p. 367. Also see Carolyn Cline, "The Image of Public Relations in Mass Comm Textbooks," *Public Relations Review*, Fall, 1982, p. 63.

4. *Business and Society Review*, Winter, 1983, p. 20.

5. Hundreds of books describe the economics of British–colonial relations during the prerevolutionary era. For a good recent discussion of what the Constitution framers were rebelling against, see Marc F. Plattner, "American Democracy and the Acquisitive Spirit," in Robert A. Goldwin and William A. Schambra, eds., *How Capitalistic is the Constitution?* (Washington: American Enterprise Institute, 1982), pp. 1–21.

6. See *The Federalist Papers*, in many editions. Working out of the New American Library edition (1961), the following pages are particularly worth examination: Fed. 7, p. 65; Fed. 10, pp. 78, 83–84; Fed. 12, p. 91; Fed. 37, p. 227; Fed. 44, pp. 281–283; Fed. 51, pp. 322–325; Fed. 56, p. 349; Fed. 85, pp. 521–522.

7. Ibid.

CHAPTER ONE
Voluntarism and Restraint

1. Alan Raucher, *Public Relations and Business, 1900–1929* (Baltimore: The Johns Hopkins Press, 1968), p. 1.

2. See Elizabeth White, *American Opinion of France* (New York: Knopf, 1927), particularly pp. 80ff.

3. *Norfolk and Portsmouth Herald*, March 4, 1825, p. 2.

4. Ibid., p. 2.

5. *The Carolina Observer*, March 10, 1825, p. 2.

6. *Charleston City Gazette*, March 19, 1825, p. 2.

7. Edgar Brandon, *A Pilgrimage of Liberty* (Athens, Ohio: The Lawhead Press, 1944), p. 90.

8. Sketch by Dr. Maurice Moore, quoted in Brandon, p. 60.

9. Howard Marraro, *American Opinion on the Unification of Italy* (New York: Columbia University Press, 1932), p. 5; *Proceedings of the Public Demonstration of Sympathy with Pope Pius IX, and with Italy, 1847* (New York: H. Nelson Gay, 1847), p. 1.

10. P. Harvey Middleton, *Railways and Public Opinion* (Chicago: Railway Business Association, 1941), p. 8.

11. Ibid., p. 17.

12. Alexis de Tocqueville, *Democracy in America* (New York: Vintage, 1945), Volume II, pp. 114, 116.

13. De Tocqueville, Volume I, pp. 315–316.

14. Amos Kendall, *Autobiography* (Boston: Ticknor, 1902), p. 175.

15. Claude G. Bowers, *The Party Battles of the Jackson Period* (Boston: Houghton Mifflin, 1922), p. 147.

16. *Georgetown (Kentucky) Patriot*, April 20, 1816.

17. As one of Barnum's less-quoted lines put it, "the public is wiser than many imagine." Barnum's autobiography is available in many editions and is stimulating reading; also see M. R. Werner *Barnum* (New York: Harcourt Brace, 1923); and Neil Harris, *Humbug* (Boston: Little, Brown, 1973); as well as Blaine McKee, "P. T. Barnum: Master Publicist," *Public Relations Journal*, October, 1972.

18. Daniel Boorstin, *The Image, or What Happened to the American Dream* (New York: Antheneum, 1962), p. 210.

19. Hugh Smith, *The Theory and Regulation of Public Sentiment*, 1842, quoted in letter from J. Carroll Bateman to George M. Crowdon, assistant to the president, Illinois Central Railroad, January 15, 1957. Bateman papers, Barker Texas History Center, The University of Texas.

20. *The Washington Monthly*, May, 1975, p. 14.

21. Henry Steele Commager, *The American Mind* (New Haven: Yale University Press, 1954), pp. 30–31.

CHAPTER TWO
Onto the Gravy Train

1. Winthrop M. Daniels, *American Railroads* (Princeton: Princeton University Press, 1932), p. 9; Thomas C. Cochran, *Railroad Leaders, 1845–1890* (Cambridge: Harvard University Press, 1953), p. 266. Other books with useful information about the railroad industry during this period include Carter Goodrich, *Government Promotion of American Canals and Railroads, 1800–1890* (New York: Columbia University Press, 1960); James F. Hudson, *The Railways and the Republic* (New York: Harper & Brothers, 1887); Frank Parsons, *The Railways, the Trusts, and the People* (Philadelphia: Equity, 1905); Gabriel Kolko, *Railroads and Regulation, 1877–1916* (Princeton: Princeton University Press, 1965); Lee Benson, *Merchants, Farmers and Railroads* (Cambridge: Harvard University Press, 1955); Arthur Johnson and Barry Supple, *Boston Capitalists and Western Railroads* (Cambridge: Harvard University Press, 1967); Frederick Cleveland and Fred Powell, *Railroad Promotion and Capitalization in the United States* (New York: Longmans, Green & Co., 1909); and George Miller, *Railroads and the Granger Laws* (Madison: The University of Wisconsin Press, 1971). Cochran's book is not only an interesting secondary source but a useful primary source because of its extensive appendix, which includes letters of railroad industry leaders.

2. Johnson and Supple, p. 137; Goodrich, p. 172.

3. Goodrich, p. 171.

4. Ibid., p. 185.

5. Letter from Cass to J. B. Black, January 25, 1873. Also see Cass to C. D. Wiley, February 20, 1873; to Jay Cooke, June 17, 1873. Archives of the Northern Pacific Railroad, St. Paul, Minn., with all other Cass material cited, along with materials from Robert Harris. Reprinted in Cochran, p. 285.

6. Cass to Benjamin Wade, December 1, 1874; to C. W. Mead, April 5, 1875; to William Moorhead, January 15, 1875. Cass was frequently frustrated at the Northern Pacific as Jay Cooke and others increased their "lobbying" expenditures over his objections. He told Moorhead, "Day after day after exhausting my wits to save the Co. sums as small as five dollars, to have Bills presented by which thieves scoop the Company's Treasury of sums of tens of thousands, is too discouraging for me to stand . . . The cure for all evils that threaten this Co. seems to be a prodigal disbursement of money for which no services are rendered."

7. Perkins to William Baldwin, December 7, 1886. Chicago, Burlington & Quincy Railroad Archives, Newberry Library, Chicago, Illinois. This letter (p. 445) and other materials from CB&Q Archives are reprinted in Cochran.

8. Ledyard to W. J. Spicer, June 30, 1885. Archives of the Michigan Central Railroad, Detroit, Michigan, with all other Ledyard material cited. Reprinted in Cochran, p. 377. Under pooling systems, private deals could also be arranged; for instance, Robert Harris, president of the Chicago, Burlington & Quincy, would simply write to Charles Francis Adams, Jr., when he was president of Union Pacific. "We are willing to surrender St. Louis altogether, your Company surrendering Milwaukee." (February 20, 1885). But collaboration proved frustrating to railroading enthusiasts who wanted every road to be a good road. In a revealing letter, John Griswold, director of the Chicago, Burlington and Quincy, noted concerning purchase of a competitor, "When we bought this Road it was understood that we did so to prevent competition . . . What I fear is that our employees will get the idea that it must be put in the best condition in order to do credit to CB&Q. We bought the Road merely to get rid of competition and not with the view of adding a first class Road to our Line." (Griswold to Robert Harris, January 4, 1878, Chicago, Burlington & Quincy Archives.)

9. Ledyard to O. W. Ruggles, January 16, 1886.

10. Quoted in Alfred McClung Lee, *The Daily Newspaper in America* (New York: Macmillan, 1937), p. 436.

11. Kimball to Henry Fink, July 25, 1881. Reprinted in Cochran, p. 370.

12. Ackerman to J. F. Duncombe, n.d., 1876. Archives of the Illinois Central Railroad, Newberry Library, Chicago, with all other Ackerman material cited. Reprinted in Cochran, p. 234.

13. Ackerman to Duncombe, February 5, 1878; Ackerman to William Osborn, August 28, 1880. Ackerman personally attempted to convince academic skeptics. Such was his ideological belief in collaboration that he appeared truly uncomprehending when the Burlington line, seeing an opportunity to compete, seized it: "We have always supposed that we could count on the Burlington Company as a friendly ally to maintain rates . . . We feel that this business from Gibson South justly belongs to the Illinois Central and we cannot understand what motive could prompt" Burlington "to snatch this business away from us."

14. Ackerman to Charles Perkins, November 11, 1881; to Osborn, March 3, 1881.

15. Brisbin to Samuel Sloan, quoted in Cochran, p. 195; Denison to Robert Harris, February 22, 1873, Chicago, Burlington & Quincy Archives.

16. Ledyard to Rt. Rev. George Worthington, March 22, 1886.

17. Ackerman to L. V. F. Randolph, December 29, 1880.

18. Ackerman to William Osborn, August 20, 1878; Ackerman to S. Fish, February 20, 1883.

19. Brooks to George Harris, March 9, 1871. Chicago, Burlington & Quincy Archives.

20. The New York Times, Feb. 22, 1881, p. 1.

21. Ibid.

22. Ledyard to A. L. Osborne, February 3, 1883.

23. Ackerman to L. V. F. Randolph, March 3, 1879.

24. Forbes to Charles Perkins, September 12, 1885; Chicago, Burlington & Quincy Archives, along with all other Forbes and Perkins material.

25. Forbes to William C. Endicott, Jr., January 29, 1887.

26. A previous version of my railroad public relations analysis appeared in Journalism Monographs #102, Association for Education in Journalism and Mass Communication, 1987.

CHAPTER THREE
Railroad Executives and the Interstate Commerce Commission

1. Harris to J. Sterling Morton, July 21, 1877.

2. Ibid.

3. Perkins to Thomas J. Potter, January 5, 1887; Perkins to Forbes, April 28, 1878. Adams quoted in Gabriel Kolko, Railroads and Regulation, 1877–1916 (Princeton: Princeton University Press, 1965), p. 37. Perkins was a pessimistic mugwump among railroad executives. While he saw regulation as "inevitable," he also saw it leading to disaster. In 1885 he wrote to railroad bridge engineer George Morison, "The mistake the railroads are in danger of making is that they think they can modify public opinion by admitting the necessity of some legislation, hoping to be able to guide it . . . " To the president of the Pennsylvania Railroad, George Roberts, Perkins wrote, "We may be forced, as you suggest, to accept legislation by Congress, but as I believe that all such legislation must fail in the end in the accomplishment of any good object, I can see nothing to gain in an attempt to guide it. Will not any such attempt on the part of the railroads probably result in worse legislation than we shall be likely to get if the railroads stand up squarely and insist that Congress should do nothing, giving, as they can, good reasons for their position." (August 3, 1885). But Perkins ended up believing that the locomotive of history was speeding down the tracks, beyond his control.

4. Perkins to Forbes, April 28, 1878; Ackerman to L. V. F. Randolph, March 5, 1881.

5. Rocky Mountain News, March 8, 1881, p. 1.

6. Reason, October, 1984, p. 40.

7. Perkins to George S. Morison, August 3, 1885; Treasury Department, *Report on the Internal Commerce of the United States*, 1879, p. 190.

8. Adams quoted in Kolko, p. 37; George Blanchard, *Traffic Unity, Popularly Called 'Railway Pools'* (New York: Erie, 1884), pp. 30, 34.

9. The *New York Times*, February 26, 1882, pp. 1–2; New York *Tribune*, February 26, 1882, p. 1.

10. The *New York Times*, August 15, 1881, p. 4; August 17, p. 4.

11. *New York Tribune*, February 4, 1881, p. 4; November 25, 1881, p. 4.

12. Ibid.

13. *Atlanta Constitution*, October 18, 1881, p. 1; *Kaufman Sun*, June 3, 1881, p. 2; *Rocky Mountain News*, March 8, 1881, p. 1.

14. *Chicago Tribune*, March 1, 1881, p. 12; March 3, p. 12; March 8, p. 12.

15. *Chicago Tribune*, July 6, 1881, p. 7; March 3, 1881, p. 12; July 1, 1881, p. 4; August 2, 1881, p. 6.

16. Perkins to Forbes, June 11, 1885.

17. U.S. House of Representatives, Committee on Commerce, *Hearings*, 48:1, pp. 1–2.

18. Ibid., p. 39.

19. U.S. Senate, Select Committee on Interstate Commerce, Senate Report No. 46.

20. For these quotations and the full debate, see 17 *Congressional Record*, XVII, 49:1. Also quoted in Robert E. Cushman, *The Indpendent Regulatory Commission* (London: Oxford University Press), pp. 56–58.

21. See 18 *Congressional Record*, Appendix. Quoted in Cushman, p. 51.

22. William P. Shinn, "The Relations of Railways to the State," *Railway Review*, March 13, 1886, pp. 121–122.

23. Reprinted in *Public Opinion*, January 8, 1887, p. 249.

24. See Kolko, pp. 45–63 for an excellent discussion of the formative years of the Interstate Commerce Commission, 1887–1890.

25. Ibid, p. 52.

26. Lee Benson, *Merchants, Farmers, and Railroads* (Cambridge: Harvard University Press, 1955), p. 241.

27. Albro Martin, *Enterprise Denied: Origins of the Decline of American Railroads, 1897–1917* (New York: Columbia University Press, 1971), p. xii.

28. Ray Stannard Baker, "Railroads on Trial," *McClures*, September, 1905, p. 537.

CHAPTER FOUR
Two-Front War

1. For discussion of general developments in public relations during this era, see Alan Raucher, *Public Relations and Business, 1900–1929* (Baltimore: Johns Hopkins, 1968), and Richard Tedlow, *Keeping the Corporate Image* (Greenwich, Conn: JAI Press, 1979).

2. My interpretation of the Progressive Era particularly reflects insights of Robert H. Wiebe, *Businessmen and Reform: A Study of the Progressive Movement* (Cambridge:

Harvard University Press, 1962), and Herbert Schlossberg, *Idols for Destruction* (Nashville: Thomas Nelson, 1983). Two books from the political left also provide useful descriptions, although I cannot agree with the authors' prescriptions: Gabriel Kolko, *The Triumph of Conservatism* (New York: Macmillan Co., 1963), and James Weinstein, *The Corporate Ideal in the Liberal State, 1900–1918* (Boston: Beacon Press, 1968).

3. The most complete portrayal of Insull is in Forest McDonald, *Insull* (Chicago: The University of Chicago Press, 1962).

4. See Samuel Insull, *Central-Station Electric Service: Its Commercial Development and Economic Significance as Set Forth in Public Address, 1897–1914* (Chicago: Privately printed, 1915).

5. Ibid.

6. See Robert W. Poole, ed., *Unnatural Monopolies: The Case for Deregulating Public Utilities* (Santa Barbara, Ca: The Reason Foundation, 1985).

7. McDonald, p. 117.

8. Ibid.

9. Ibid, pp. 116–117.

10. See Samuel Insull, *Public Utilities in Modern Life: Selected Speeches, 1914–1923* (Chicago: Privately printed, 1924).

11. Bureau of the Census, *Telephones: 1907* (Washington, D.C.: Bureau of Commerce and Labor, 1910).

12. See Harry B. MacMeal, *The Story of Independent Telephony* (Chicago: (Independent Pioneer Telephone Association, 1934), and Albert Bigelow Paine, *Theodore N. Vail* (New York: Harper and Bros., 1921).

13. John Brooks, *Telephone: The First Hundred Years* (New York: Harper & Row, 1975), pp. 109–110.

14. MacMeal, pp. 204–210; Brooks, p. 136.

15. Brooks, p. 112.

16. Ibid., p. 113.

17. Raucher, p. 49.

18. See Vail's report on "Public Relations" in Theodore Vail, *Views on Public Questions: A Collection of Papers and Addresses of Theodore Newton Vail, 1907–1917* (New York: Privately printed, 1917), pp. 5–12.

19. Ibid., pp. 114, 115.

20. Ibid., pp. 117, 118.

21. George V. S. Michaelis, "Is Municipal Ownership a Dream?" *Moody's Magazine*, October, 1906, pp. 538–541.

22. N. R. Danielian, *AT&T* (New York: Vanguard Press, 1939), pp. 291–333; Vail, pp. 111–135.

23. Ernest Gruening, *The Public Pays* (New York: Vanguard Press, 1931), p. 190; Danielian, pp. 308–315. Gruening, a magazine journalist during the 1920s who became a U.S. Senator from Alaska during the 1960s (and an early critic of American involvement in Vietnam), was a close observer of public relations. He reviewed Edward Bernays' first book, *Crystallizing Public Opinion*, and demanded honesty in public statements by both others and himself. *The Public Pays* received considerable attention and critical praise when it was published; its findings have never been refuted.

24. Bernard J. Mullaney, "Establishing Public Relations," *Gas Age Record*, October 28, 1922, p. 577; Gruening, p. 19. Also see Insull, *Public Utilities in Modern Life* (Chicago: Privately printed, 1924).

25. Federal Communications Commission, *Control of Telephone Communications, Volume IV: Politics of Control (Exhibit 2096-E)*, p. 38.

26. Ibid., p. 39; Danielian, p. 311.

27. Quoted in Jack Levin, *Power Ethics* (New York: Knopf, 1931), p. 41. Levin was on the research staff of "People's Legislative Service," an early equivalent of Nader's Raiders. A check of his quotations against original sources, when available, shows that he was thorough and reliable, not taking quotations out of context. His goal was to "analyze the activities of the private utilities in their information committees and bureaus to determine their aims, the agencies through which they function, and the kind of work they engage in . . ." (pp. 168–169). He succeeded admirably, but his work was marketed less effectively than that of Gruening and seemed to receive less attention. For a summary of other utility public relations efforts, see Congress, Senate, *Utility Corporations: Efforts by Associations and Agencies of Electric and Gas Utilities to Influence Public Opinion, A Summary Report Prepared by the Federal Trade Commission*, 70th Congress, first session, 1934, Senate Document 92, part 71-A.

28. Gruening, pp. 162, 163.

29. FCC, pp. 39, 45–48.

30. Sheridan's statements in FTC Exhibit Parts 5 & 6, p. 228. Also found in Carl D. Thompson, *Confessions of the Power Trust* (New York: Dutton, 1932), pp. 283–286, 318–319, and Gruening, pp. 165, 166.

31. Campaign summarized in Levin, pp. 100–105. Quotation in Greuning, p. 166. See also Thompson, pp. 309–319, for criticism of Insull-Mullaney activities.

32. Gruening, pp. 181, 187.

33. Gruening, p. 171; Levin, pp. 106–111.

34. Levin, pp. 112–122; Gruening, p. 183.

35. Gruening, pp. 203–204.

36. Thompson, pp. 437–443.

37. Ibid.; Gruening, p. 126.

38. FTC Exhibit Parts 5 & 6, p. 155; Thompson pp. 415–416; Levin, pp. 147–166; Gruening, p. 119.

39. Gruening, p. 227.

40. Thompson, pp. 330–359; Levin, pp. 70–74; Gruening, p. 118.

41. Thompson, pp. 360–392; Levin, pp. 75–80; Gruening, p. 93.

42. Gruening, p. 64; Levin, pp. 81–86.

43. FTC, pp. 92–98, 104–105; Raucher, p. 85.

44. Danielian, p. 277. See also George Griswold, Jr., "How AT&T Public Relations Policies Developed," *Public Relations Quarterly*, Fall, 1967, and Noel L. Griese, "He Walked in the Shadows: Public Relations Counsel Arthur W. Page," *Public Relations Quarterly*, Fall, 1976.

45. FTC, Exhibit parts 5 & 6, pp. 306–7; Thompson, p. 9.

46. Ibid.; Thompson, p. 11.

47. Ibid, p. 156; Thompson, p. 13.

48. Gruening, p. 247.

CHAPTER FIVE
The Work of Ivy Lee

1. Public-relations minded executives were only one of the groups agitating for a greater governmental role in private enterprise. The Socialist Party, for instance, gained considerable strength early in the century. But once the federal government was seen as a possible source of corporate economic gain, demands for subsidy and monopolistic privileges began increasing. A new view of government–corporate relationships was particularly evident in the work of the National Civic Federation, which in 1903 included representatives of over one third of the 367 corporations with a capitalization of over $10 million, and was designed to help the corporation become "no longer merely a private institution" but "a wholesome center in which a large part of the living of society was becoming concentrated." Robert H. Wiebe, *Businessmen and Reform: A Study of the Progressive Movement* (Cambridge: Harvard University Press, 1962), p. 20.

2. Lee's "Declaration of Principles" is quoted in Scott Cutlip and Allen Center, *Effective Public Relations*, revised fifth edition (Englewood Cliffs, N.J.: Prentice-Hall, 1982), p. 79. Reporters' views are noted in Henry F. Pringle, "His Master's Voice," *The American Mercury*, October, 1926, p. 151. Carl Sandburg may have been the original popularizer of the nickname, "Poison Ivy." Chapter 48 of Upton Sinclair's bitter book, *The Brass Check* (Pasadena, Ca.: Published by the Author, 1920), is entitled "Poison Ivy."

3. The standard biography of Lee is Ray Hiebert, *Courtier to the Crowd* (Ames, Iowa: Iowa State University Press, 1966). Brief examinations of Lee may be found in Alan Raucher, *Public Relations and Business, 1900–1929* (Baltimore: Johns Hopkins, 1968); Richard Tedlow, *Keeping the Corporate Image* (Greenwich, Conn: JAI Press, 1979); Eric Goldman, *Two-way Street: The Emergence of the Public Relations Counsel* (Boston: Bellman, 1948).

4. From 1895 to 1904, an average of 301 companies with a total capitalization of $691 million disappeared each year. While companies were merging, company "welfare programs" were growing, with a National Civic Foundation survey showing 2,500 practicing "corporate paternalists" in 1914.

5. See Gabriel Kolko, *The Triumph of Conservatism* (New York: Macmillan, 1963), p. 5.

6. U.S. Industrial Commission, Preliminary Report, Vol. 5, p. 797; Kolko, p. 64.

7. Wiebe, p. 204.

8. *North American Review*, CLXXII (1901), p. 647.

9. Ibid., p. 649.

10. *Annals of the American Academy of Political and Social Science*, 1912, p. 126. Quoted in Kolko, p. 14.

11. See, for instance, James Hudson, *The Railway and the Republic* (New York: Harper & Brothers, 1887).

12. Hiebert, p. 29.

13. *New York Times*, March 27, 1933, p. 16.

14. Kolko, p. 14.

15. Peter Collier and David Horowitz, *The Rockefellers* (New York: Holt, Rinehart and Winston, 1976), p. 152.

16. See Ivy Lee, *Human Nature and Railroads* (Philadelphia: Nash, 1915); Ivy Lee, *Present-Day Russia* (New York: Macmillan, 1928); Ivy Lee, "Higher Fares Benefit the Public," *Electric Railway Journal*, September 15, 1917, p. 441; Ivy Lee, "Some Practical Aspects of the Railroad Problem," *Academy of Political Science Proceedings*, January, 1920, pp. 703–706; Silas Bent, "Ivy Lee: Minnesinger to Millionaires," *New Republic*, November 29, 1929, pp. 369–372.

17. Ivy Lee, "The Human Nature of Publicity," *Electric Railway Journal*, August 4, 1917, p. 182; Ivy Lee, *Publicity for Private Service Corporations* (New York: privately printed, 1916); quoted in Hiebert, p. 72. Freudianism became popular among intellectuals during this period, particularly after Freud himself came to the United States and spoke at Clark University in 1909. Others were influenced also: Walter Lippmann, for one, accepted the new view of man and, as early as 1912, began to think about its implications for politics. Popularized Freudianism swept the country during Lee's years of greatest influence. How-to volumes such as *The Psychology of Package Labels* and *The Psychology of Selling Life Insurance* were eagerly read by businessmen and others.

18. Collier and Horowitz, p. 117.

19. Jacques Ellul, *Propaganda* (New York: Vintage, 1973), p. 53. Lee was very timely in his espousal of changing ethics. Roderick Nash has concluded that "The American idea of human nature underwent a striking transformation between 1910 and 1925. Psychology provided the theoretical framework for the new view." Merle Curti found that *Printers' Ink* articles moved in about 1910 from the concept of man as a rational creature capable of spotting lies to that in which men could be swayed by attention-getting stimuli and appeals to the senses.

20. Hiebert, p. 178. Lee performed similar chores for many clients, and sometimes even developed synergistic programs. Working in 1923 for both The Copper and Brass Research Association and John D. Rockefeller, who was helping to fund work on the Cathedral of St. John the Divine, Lee wrote an article describing the cathedral and pointing out that many important pipes and other parts were made of copper, "a metal whose worthiness had been proved by its centuries of service on churches and cathedrals in England and on the Continent." (Raucher, p. 99)

21. Ibid., p. 177.

22. Ivy Lee, "An Open and Above-Board Trust," *Moody's Magazine*, June, 1907, pp. 158–164.

23. Ivy Lee, "Indirect Service of Railroads," *Moody's Magazine*, November, 1907, pp. 580–584.

24. Cutlip and Center, p. 79.

25. Tedlow, p. 37; Hiebert, p. 101. Lee did receive great abuse at this time; Sandburg called him a "paid liar," and his Ludlow activity "dirty work. It was coarse. It was cheap. It was desperately bold and overplayed . . . Ivy Lee is below the level of the hired gunman and slugger. His sense of right and wrong is a worse force in organized society than that of the murderers . . ."

26. *Business Week*, June 29, 1930, p. 35.

27. Lee, "Relationships to the Russian Problem," *Annals of the American Academy of Political and Social Science*, July, 1928, p. 93.

28. *Business Week*, op. cit.

29. Lee, *Present-Day Russia*, pp. 153–156.

30. *Business Week*, op. cit.

31. New York *Times*, March 29, 1926, p. 1.

32. Hiebert, p./273.

33. New York *Times*, October 29, 1930, p. 14.

34. New York *Times*, February 22, 1929, p. 8.

35. Hiebert, p. 307.

36. A previous version of chapters 4 and 5 appeared in *Journalism Monographs* #102, Association for Education in Journalism and Mass Communication, 1987.

CHAPTER SIX
The Movie Industry Gets a Czar

1. Will H. Hays, *The Memoirs of Will H. Hays* (Garden City, New York: Doubleday, 1955), p. 351, concerning the movie industry: "I question whether any other industry has ever made such a record of organizing good will in its support on so large a scale."

2. See, for instance, N.Y. Laws, 1921, C. 715; Fla. Gen. Laws, 1921, C. 8523; Md. Laws, 1916, C. 209; Photoplay Corporation v. Board of Review, 102 Kansas 356 (1918). Also see "Official Censorship Legislation" in *Annals of the American Academy of Political and Social Science* (November, 1926).

3. Howard T. Lewis, *The Motion Picture Industry* (New York: D. Van Nostrand, 1933) includes an extended discussion of the industry's economic relationships, p. 388.

4. See pamphlet, *A Survey of the Motion Picture Problem* (New York: Federal Motion Picture Council of America, 1925); Raymond Moley, *The Hays Office* (Indianapolis: Bobbs-Merrill, 1945), pp. 32-35; and Terry Ramsaye, *A Million and One Nights* (New York: Simon and Schuster, 1926), p. 815.

5. Edmund G. Lowry, *Washington Close-Ups* (Boston: Houghton Mifflin, 1921), p. 34.

6. Pamphlet, *By-Laws of Motion Picture Producers and Distributors of America, Inc.* (New York: MPPDA, 1922); Hays, pp. 323-327.

7. Moley, p. 37.

8. Hays, pp. 342, 349-350.

9. Ibid., p. 428.

10. Ibid., p. 430.

11. See *Annual Report to the Motion Picture Producers and Distributors of America, Inc.*, by Will H. Hays, 1923.

12. Ramsaye, pp. 818-819.

13. Pamphlet, *The Public Relations of the Motion Picture Industry* (New York: Federal Council of the Churches of Christ in America, 1931); Hays, p. 338. Also see *Annual Report*, 1923.

14. "MPPDA Formula," included in Moley pp., 58-59; Hays, p. 430.

15. Hays, p. 434.

16. Hays, pp. 438, 444.

17. Pamphlet, *Code to Govern the Making of Talking, Synchronized and Silent Motion Pictures* (New York: Motion Picture Producers and Distributors of America, 1930).

18. Moley, p. 75.

19. Lewis, p. 388.

20. Ibid., p. 389.

21. Martin Quigley, *Decency in Motion Pictures* (New York: Macmillan, 1937).

22. Ibid., p. 32.

23. Ibid., p. 37.

24. Ibid., p. 38.

25. See "Whither the Movies?" in *Motion Picture Monthly*, April–May 1931, p. 51.

26. Hays, pp. 444, 446.

27. *A Survey of the Motion Picture Problem* (New York: Federal Motion Picture Council of America, 1924), p. 5.

28. Ibid. Also see pamphlet by William Sheafe Chase, *Is the Trend of Motion Pictures Upward?* (New York: Federal Motion Picture Council of America, 1926).

29. Hays, pp. 347–348.

30. *The Literary Digest*, June 23, 1934, p. 19.

31. Fred Eastman, "Ambassadors of Good Will," *Christian Century*, January 29, 1930, pp. 145–146; *Christian Century*, June 7, 1933, p. 750.

32. *Christian Century*, April 13, 1932, p. 482.

33. *Harrison's Reports*, May 7, 1933, p. 3.

34. *Christian Science Monitor*, January 24, 1933, p. 4.

35. *The Churchman*, July 13, 1929, p. 5; *The Literary Digest*, September 21, 1929, p. 15.

36. Pamphlet, *Broken Promises of the Motion Picture Industry* (New York: International Reform Federation, 1929); "Federal Council of Churches—Critic," *Motion Picture Monthly*, June-July, 1931, p. 2.

37. *Child Welfare*, January, 1933, p. 2.

38. *Annual Report*, 1934.

39. Hays, pp. 447–448.

40. *Motion Picture Magazine*, November, 1934, p. 31.

41. Hays, p. 451.

42. *New York Times*, July 21, 1934, p. 14; June 15, 1934, p. 19; June 20, 1934, p. 23; June 16, 1934, p. 13; July 30, 1934, p.9; September 28, 1934, p. 27; October 7, 1934, p. 32; October 24, 1934, p. 13; November 25, 1934, Section IV, p. 7; November 24, 1934, Section IX, p. 5; August 5, 1934, Section IX, p. 2; June 19, 1934, p. 24; June 27, 1934, p. 21; July 4, 1934, p. 16; July 2, 1934, p. 24; July 10, 1934, p. 19; August 10, 1934, p. 21; November 28, 1934, p. 25.

43. Paul W. Facey, *The Legion of Decency* (New York: Arno Press, 1974), p. 55.

44. Facey, p. 60.

45. Ibid., and *Christian Century*, June 20, 1934, p. 822.

46. *Motion Picture Magazine*, October, 1934, p. 85; John McCarthy, "Man of Decency," *Esquire*, September, 1935, p. 126.

47. Facey, p. 151.

48. Jack Vizzard, *See No Evil* (New York: Simon and Schuster, 1970), p. 50.

49. *Annual Report*, 1935, 1938.

50. Hays, pp. 452–454.

51. *Esquire*, September, 1935, p. 64.

52. Ibid.

53. Vizzard, p. 51.

54. Ibid., p. 52.

55. Ibid., p. 53.

56. Robert Sklar, *Movie-Made America* (New York: Random House, 1975), p. 175. Also see Hortense Powdermaker, *Hollywood: The Dream Factory* (Boston: Little, Brown, 1950), pp. 65, 81.

CHAPTER SEVEN
Corporate PR and the National Recovery Administration

1. Robert Himmelberg, *The Origins of the National Recovery Administration* (New York: Fordham University Press, 1976), p. 116; Charles R. Stevenson, *The Way Out* (New York: Privately printed, 1932), pp. 3-4, 25-33.

2. Gerard Swope, *The Swope Plan*, edited by J. G. Frederick (New York: The Business Course, 1931), p. 159.

3. Ibid.

4. Ellis Hawley, *The New Deal and the Problem of Monopoly* (Princeton: Princeton U. Press, 1966), p. 41.

5. Himmelberg, p. 159.

6. Barnes to Chapin, April 20, 1931, Roy Chapin Papers, The University of Michigan.

7. Himmelberg, p. 135.

8. Swope, p. 58.

9. Himmelberg, pp. 185, 187.

10. Butler Shaffer, *In Restraint of Trade: Business Attitudes Toward Competition and Regulation, 1918-1938*, unpublished manuscript, p. 3-55.

11. Ibid.

12. *Business Week*, May 17, 1933, p. 3.

13. Ibid.

14. *New York Times*, April 28, 1933, p. 14; June 17, p. 2.

15. *Wall Street Journal*, May 5, 1933, pp. 2, 3.

16. *New York Times*, May 16, 1933, p. 23.

17. *Iron Age*, 1933, pp. 484, 907.

18. *Business Week*, May 10, 1933, p. 32; also see *Textile World*, May, 1933, pp. 901-902.

19. See Shaffer, chapter four, "Under the Blue Eagle and Beyond"; *Business Week*, June 7, 1933; Hawley, p. 57.

20. Broadus Mitchell, *Depression Decade* (New York: Rinehart and Co., 1947), p. 243.

21. Shaffer, op. cit.

22. Hawley, pp. 56-57; Lewis L. Lorwin and A. Ford Hinrichs, *National Economic and Social Planning* (Washington: General Printing Office, 1935), pp. 71, 85.

23. Hawley, p. 83.

24. *New York Times*, September 14, 1933, p. 1.

25. *The Rotarian*, July, 1936, p. 14; *Baltimore Sun*, July 3, 1933, included in Frank Kent, *Without Gloves* (New York: William Morrow, 1934), p. 35.

26. Alfred Lief, *The Firestone Story*, (New York: Whittlesey House, 1951), pp. 198–203; New York *Times*, June 8, 1933, p. 29; *Wall Street Journal*, June 9, 1933, p. 13.

27. Lief, pp. 198–203; Cabell Phillips, *From the Crash to the Blitz* (New York: Macmillan, 1969), p. 221.

28. *Wall Street Journal*, May 20, 1933, p. 1; *Business Week*, June 24, 1933, p. 12.

29. Himmelberg, p. 205; Albert Romasco, *The Politics of Recovery* (New York and London: Oxford University Press, 1983), p. 200.

30. Hugh Johnson, *The Blue Eagle from Egg to Earth* (Garden City: Doubleday, Doran, 1935), pp. 169, 171, 262; *American Magazine*, August, 1934, p. 21.

31. Romasco, p. 200.

32. Shaffer, p. 4–12.

33. Herman Krooss, *Executive Opinion* (Garden City, N.Y.: Doubleday, 1970), p. 172; *Business Week*, Sept. 16, 1933, p. 8.

34. *Wall Street Journal*, August 31, 1933, p. 2.

35. Phillips, p. 220.

36. Hawley, p. 54; Phillips, p. 221.

37. *Wall Street Journal*, September 14, 1933, p. 9; *Current History*, October, 1933, pp. 78–81; *Saturday Evening Post*, December 2, 1933, p. 10; Raymond Moley, *The First New Deal* (New York: Harcourt, Brace & World, 1966), p. 15.

38. *Wall Street Journal*, September 14, 1933, p. 9; December 2, 1933, p. 2.

39. Johnson, p. 301. Unsurprisingly, the conception of critics as Judases brought out "love it or leave it" arguments from opponents. Donald Richberg said that critics should simply "emigrate to some backward country." Frank Kent noted that presidential prestige and "Blue Eagle ballyhoo reduced those who opposed to almost complete silence." Kent, *Without Gloves*, p. 107.

40. Johnson, p. 263.

41. Ibid., p. 265.

42. Charles L. Dearing et. al., *The ABC of the NRA* (Wash: Brookings, 1934), pp. 745, 788, 828, 851–3, 873. Hawley observed that starting in the fall of 1933 "the realization began to draw that essentially the codes reflected the interests of the larger and more highly organized businessmen, that the NRA was busily promoting cartels in the interest of scarcity profits." (p. 66).

43. *New York Times*, Jan. 11, 19, 20, 1934; *Time*, Jan. 29, 1934, p. 14.

44. Ibid., Feb. 3, 7, 8, 21, 22, 1934.

45. *Baltimore Sun*, January 20, 1934, included in Kent, *Without Gloves*, p. 158.

46. *New York Times*, January 18, 1935, p. 4; March 14, p. 1; March 15, p. 40; March 20, p. 43; March 21, p. 41; March 22, pp. 15, 38; March 26, p. 37; March 28, p. 6; April 18, p. 33; May 3, p. 26; May 7, p. 15; May 16, p. 2; May 18, p. 2; May 24, p. 40; May 27, p. 13. Hawley, pp. 114–115.

47. Johnson, pp. 377–408.

48. *New York Times*, May 23, 1935, p. 1; May 26, 1935, sec. 4, p. 10; May 2, 1935, p. 38.

49. *New York Times*, May 2, 1935, p. 2.

50. *Wall Street Journal*, May 28, p. 1.

51. Ibid., May 31, p. 2.

CHAPTER EIGHT
The Public Relations Theory of Edward Bernays

1. Proceedings, National Association of Manufacturers, 1922.

2. Charles Fay, *Business in Politics* (Cambridge, Mass: The Cosmos Press, 1926), p. 25.

3. *Nation's Business*, April, 1933, pp. 12, 20.

4. *Saturday Evening Post*, May, 1934, p. 27.

5. Edward L. Bernays, *Propaganda* (New York: Liveright, 1928).

6. Ibid., p. 159.

7. Ray Eldon Hiebert, *Courtier to the Crowd: The Story of Ivy Lee and the Development of Public Relations* (Ames, Iowa: Iowa State University Press, 1966), p. 87.

8. Interview conducted at 7 Lowell Street, Cambridge, Mass., August 10, 1984.

9. Edward L. Bernays, *Biography of an Idea: Memoirs of Public Relations Counsel Edward L. Bernays* (New York: Simon and Schuster, 1965), p. 8.

10. See Bernays, "Manipulating Public Opinion: The Why and the How," *The American Journal of Sociology*, May, 1928, pp. 958-971.

11. Interview.

12. John T. Flynn, "Edward L. Bernays: The Science of Ballyhoo," *Atlantic Monthly*, May, 1931, pp. 562-571.

13. *The Nation*, February 16, 1927; quoted in Bernays, *Biography of an Idea*, p. 319.

14. Interview.

15. Ibid.

16. Bernays, *Biography of an Idea*, pp,. 62-3.

17. Ibid.

18. "Calls Bernays a 'Professional Nephew,' " *Variety*, April 19, 1961, pp. 2, 17. Cited in *Public Relations, the Edward L. Bernayses and the American Scene: A Bibliography* (Westwood, Mass: F. W. Faxon Co., 1978).

19. Bernays, *Propaganda*, p. 52.

20. Ibid., p. 52.

21. Ibid., p. 20.

22. Interview.

23. See *Propaganda* for Bernays' 1920s ideas; Bernays, ed., *The Engineering of Consent* (Norman, Oklahoma: U. of Oklahoma Press, 1955) for this similar 1950s concept.

24. Interview.

24. Ibid.

25. Walter Lippmann, *Public Opinion* (New York: Macmillan, 1945), p. 345. See also John Dewey, *Individualism Old and New* (New York: Macmillan, 1930), p. 42. Dewey continued, "The need for united action, and the supposed need for integrated opinion and sentiment, are met by organized propaganda and advertising. The publicity agent is perhaps the most significant symbol of our present social life. There are individuals who resist; but, for a time at least, sentiment can be manufactured by mass methods for almost any person or any cause."

26. Edward L. Bernays, *Crystallizing Public Opinion* (New York: Boni and Liveright, 1923), p. 111.

27. Bernays, *Propaganda*, p. 9.

28. Ibid., pp. 9–10.

29. Ibid.

30. Ibid., p. 11.

31. Ibid., p. 11–12.

32. Ibid., p. 12.

33. Ibid.

34. Ibid.

35. Ibid., p. 37. Bernays' goal was to make the manipulated act as desired, without ever realizing that they had been manipulated. One of Bernays' examples illustrates particularly well Bernays' realization that in a consumerist age with discretionary dollars yearning to be spent, the shortest distance from point *x* to point *y* might involve a tour requiring use of every letter in the alphabet: "If, for instance, I want to sell pianos, it is not sufficient to blanket the country with a direct appeal, such as: 'YOU buy a Mozart piano now. It is cheap. The best artists use it. It will last for years.' The claims may all be true, but they are in direct conflict with the claims of other piano manufacturers, and in indirect competition with the claims of a radio or a motor car, each competing for the consumer's dollar."

Instead, the public relations practitioner should "endeavor to develop public acceptance of the idea of a music room in the home. This he may do, for example, by organizing an exhibition of period music rooms designed by well known decorators who themselves exert an influence on the buying groups. He enhances the effectiveness and prestige of these rooms by putting in them rare and valuable tapestries. Then, in order to create dramatic interest in the exhibit, he stages an event or ceremony. To this ceremony key people, persons known to influence the buying habits of the public, such as a famous violinist, a popular artist, and a society leader, are invited.

"These key persons affect other groups, lifting the idea of the music room to a place in the public consciousness which it did not have before. The juxtaposition of these leaders and the idea which they are dramatizing, are then projected to the wider public through various publicity channels. Meanwhile, influential architects have been persuaded to make the music room an integral architectural part of their plans with perhaps a specially charming niche in one corner for the piano. Less influential architects will as a matter of course imitate what is done by the men whom they consider masters of their profession. They in turn will implant the idea of the music room in the mind of the general public.

"The music room will be accepted because it has been made the thing. And the man or woman who has a music room, or has arranged a corner of the parlor as a musical corner, will naturally think of buying a piano. It will come to him as his own idea. Under the old salesmanship the manufacturer said to the prospective purchaser, 'Please buy a piano.' The new salesmanship has reversed the process and caused the prospective purchaser to say to the manufacturer, 'Please sell me a piano' " (*Propaganda*, pp. 54–56).

36. Ibid., p. 37.

37. Ibid., p. 47.

38. Ibid., p. 25. Also see Bernays, "Molding Public Opinion," *The Annals of the American Academy of Political and Social Science*, May, 1935, pp. 82–87.

39. Ibid.
40. Ibid., p. 37.
41. Ibid.
42. Interview.

CHAPTER NINE
The Triumph of Manipulation

1. Bernays, "Manipulating Public Opinion: The Why and the How," *The American Journal of Sociology*, May, 1928, pp. 959.
2. Ibid.
3. *The Bookman*, April, 1924, p. 188.
4. *The Dial*, May, 1924, p. 468.
5. *Dry Goods Merchants Trade Journal*, April, 1924, p. 100. Quoted in Keith A. Larson, *Public Relations, the Edward L. Bernayses and the American Scene* (Westwood, Mass: F. W. Faxon, 1978).
6. "Turning Public Opinion Your Way," *Sales Management*, March, 1924, pp. 648, 730.
7. *The Survey*, March 15, 1924, p. 714.
8. *The Dial*, May, 1924, p. 468.
9. Ernest Gruening, "The Higher Hokum," *The Nation*, April 16, 1924, p. 450.
10. *Critic and Guide*, May, 1929, p. 197.
11. Henry Pringle, "Mass Psychologist," *The American Mercury*, February, 1930, pp. 156-157.
12. "Sea Heroes and Cigarettes," *Inquiry*, March, 1929, pp. 54-5.
13. Leon Whipple, "Letters and Life," *The Survey*, March 1, 1929, pp. 743, 747.
14. Max Freedman, ed., *Roosevelt and Frankfurter: Their Correspondence, 1928-1945* (Boston: Little, Brown, 1967), p. 214.
15. E. T. Hiller, *Principles of Sociology* (New York: Harper & Brothers, 1933), p. 621.
16. *Michigan Christian Advocate*, July 14, 1932, p. 6. Cited in Larson, p. 483.
17. *Editor & Publisher*, December 29, 1928, p. 42; September 20, 1930, p. 42; June 17, 1933, p. 40; November 11, 1933, p. 44.
18. Ibid., October 26, 1929, p. 20. Some of the frustration was explicit; on December 7, 1929, *Editor & Publisher* included the following verses: "Eddie Bernays frames it up./ Frames what up?/ Frames 'news' up./ Eddie Bernays frames 'news' up/ And makes the papers cover./ Eddie Bernays gets the cash./ Gets much cash?/ Yes, much cash./ Eddie Bernays gets large cash/ That once went into paid space." (p. 54)

Still, more than greed was at stake here. An *Editor & Publisher* editorial of September 15, 1928, referred to Bernays as the "most audacious, blatant, ponderous, insistent of the self-styled public relations counsel 'profession,'" then noted that "no matter what virtuous men Mr. Bernays or Mr. Ivy Lee or other professional propagandists may be, the device they seek to establish in public life is dangerous because it is irresponsible and is calculated to break down advertising practice, which responds to checks and balances, evolved from experience and conscience during a century of study and trial." (p. 32)

Advertising has also changed its character during the past half century, and it is now difficult to be so sanguine about its prospects, but the distinction between paid space clearly marked off as advertising matter, and public relations-created "situations of reality" which appear as news and carry the implicit third-party endorsement of a newspaper, is still a valid one.

19. *Editor & Publisher* wanted newspaper leaders to ask themselves that question. As one editorial of July 27, 1939, put it, "Perhaps someone can explain to us why it is that certain publishers who would instantly discharge a reporter for 'making news' will accept the synthetic news creations of press agents . . ." (p. 32)

20. William Harlan Hale, "Youth Uses Its Own Head," in Alfred M. Bingham and Selden Rodman, eds., *Challenge to the New Deal* (New York: Falcon Press, 1934), p. 212.

21. Ernest F. Henderson, "Public Utilities – Our 'New Deal' Devils," *Barron's Weekly*, August 12, 1935, p. 11.

22. *Opinion*, November, 1934, p. 35. In this connection *Editor & Publisher* could not resist getting off one zinger: "Eddie Bernays proposes a cabinet office of Secretary of Public Relations. Goebbels is our candidate." (February 23, 1935, p. 36).

23. *Bulletin of the Financial Advertisers Association*, July, 1935. Quoted in Larson, p. 377.

24. "Public Relations – First in the Order of Business," *Business Week*, January 23, 1937, pp. 32, 36.

25. John B. Kennedy, "The Trumpeters' Trade," *The Commentator*, December, 1938, p. 37.

26. S. H. Walker and Paul Sklar, *Business Finds Its Voice: Management's Efforts to Sell the Business Idea to the Public* (New York: Harper and Brothers, 1938), pp. 26–27.

27. *Newsweek*, February 3, 1947, p. 61.

28. "The Musician's Relation to the Public," *Etude*, April, 1936, pp. 209, 256. See also May, 1936, p. 292.

29. Maxine Block, ed., *Current Biography: Who's News and Why: 1942* (New York: H. W. Wilson, 1942), p. 76.

30. Thomas C. Cochran and William Miller, *The Age of Enterprise: A Social History of Industrial America* (New York: Macmillan, 1942), p. 310.

31. *Advertising Age*, February 21, 1944, p. 39.

32. The Bernays paradigm, like much recent liberal thought which argues that need for greater political centralization, is based on a thorough-going historicism. Bernays emphasized that in a large scale society there were only two choices: manipulation or social chaos. He saw history moving in a certain direction and public relations practitioners obligated to climb on the locomotive. Like Karl Mannheim, who did not allow for the possibility that large scale societies could avoid a central planning mechanism – for Mannheim, the choice was only between good planning and bad – so Bernays would not allow the possibility that true reality might reign; he could only emphasize that the choice was between construction of socially useful "situations of reality" and those natural realities which would lead to social chaos. In that sense he was very much in tune with Spengler, who closed his dismal book on the West's decline with the statement, "We have not the freedom to react to this or that, but the freedom to do the necessary or to do nothing. And a task that historic necessity has set *will* be accomplished with the individual or against him."

33. Bernays, *Plain Talk to Liberals* (New York: E. L. Bernays, 1945); *Take Your Place at the Peace Table* (New York: International Press, 1945).

34. *American Political Science Review*, August, 1945, pp. 818–820.

35. Ibid.

36. Ibid.

37. Edward L. Bernays, *Propaganda* (New York: Liveright, 1928), p. 20.

38. Fulton Oursler, *Behold This Dreamer! An Autobiography* (Boston: Little, Brown, 1964), p. 235. See also John T. Flynn article in *Atlantic Monthly*, May, 1932, p. 563; Flynn noted that Bernays "is a social psychologist engaged in carrying out in actual practice" powerful psychological and sociological theories, but noted the possibility that individuals "now so freely exploited for ends which they often neither see nor understand may at last become so familiar with the public relations counsel and his methods that they will stop lending themselves to manipulation."

39. J. A. R. Pimlott, *Public Relations and American Democracy* (Princeton: Princeton University Press, 1951), p. 11.

40. Daniel Boorstin, *The Image* (New York: Atheneum, 1962), p. 268.

41. *Variety*, September 21, 1960, p. 76.

CHAPTER TEN
Public Relations Adds Sugar

1. Richard Tedlow, *Keeping the Corporate Image* (Greenwich, Conn: JAI Press, 1979), p. 63.

2. S. H. Walker and Paul Sklar, *Business Finds Its Voice: Management's Effort to Sell the Business Idea to the Public* (New York: Harper and Brothers, 1938), pp. 17; Tedlow, p. 65.

3. Tedlow, p. 97.

4. Irwin Ross, *The Image Merchants* (Garden City, New Jersey: Doubleday, 1959), p. 118.

5. Ibid., p. 120.

6. Ibid., p. 121.

7. William Baldwin and Raymond Mayer, in *Public Opinion Quarterly*, Fall, 1944, p. 123.

8. See Rex Harlow, *Social Science in Public Relations* (New York: Harper and Brothers, 1957), pp. 26–27.

9. Tedlow, p. 151.

10. Ibid., p. 154.

11. Ibid.

12. For more on Garrett and Page, see L. L. L. Golden, *Only By Public Consent* (New York: Hawthorn Books, 1968), pp. 25–94 (AT&T) and 95–162 (General Motors).

13. Tedlow, p. 122.

14. Golden, pp. 163–326.

15. Ibid.

16. Ross, p. 94.

17. Constance Hope, *Publicity is Broccoli* (Indianapolis: Bobbs-Merrill, 1941), pp. 18–19.

18. *Fortune*, May, 1949, p. 196.

19. J. A. R. Pimlott, *Public Relations and American Democracy* (Princeton: Princeton University Press, 1951), p. 10.

20. Robert van Riper, *A Really Sincere Guy* (New York: David McKay, 1958), p. 123.

21. Sloan Wilson, *The Man in the Grey Flannel Suit* (New York: Simon and Schuster, 1955), p. 28.

22. Ibid., pp. 227–228.

23. Charles Yale Harrison, *Nobody's Fool* (New York: Henry Holt, 1948), p. 101.

24. Ibid., pp. 125–126.

CHAPTER ELEVEN
Last Stand for Steel

1. Most notably Wallace Carroll, "Steel: A 72-Hour Drama With an All-Star Cast," *New York Times*, April 23, 1962, p. 1; and Grant McConnell, *Steel and the Presidency, 1962* (New York: W. W. Norton, 1963).

2. *Steel*, May 8, 1933, p. 20; *New York Times*, May 16, 1933, p. 23; Byron D. Shaffer, "In Restraint of Trade: Business Attitudes Toward Competition and Regulation, 1918–1938." unpublished manuscript, p. 4–44.

3. *Steel*, June 19, 1933, p. 10.

4. Shaffer, p. 4–44.

5. Ibid., p. 4–48.

6. *Public Opinion Quarterly*, April, 1937, p. 109.

7. Ibid.

8. Richard S. Tedlow, *Keeping the Corporate Image* (Greenwich, Conn: JAI Press, 1979), pp. 102–103.

9. *Yearbook of the American Iron and Steel Institute* (New York: AISI, 1939), pp. 57, 60.

10. Ibid., p. 59.

11. Ibid., 1944, pp. 53, 55.

12. Ibid., 1946, p. 20.

13. Ibid., 1947, pp. 661.

14. Ibid., 1950, p. 55.

15. Edward L. Bernays, *Biography of an Idea* (New York: Simon & Schuster, 1965), p. 551.

16. *United States Steel Corporation Annual Report*, 1945, p. 17.

17. Ibid., 1949, p. 21.

18. Ibid., 1950, p. 20.

19. Ibid., 1955, p. 20; 1956, p. 22.

20. Ibid.

21. M. A. Adelman, "Steel, Administered Prices, and Inflation," *Quarterly Journal of Economics*, February, 1961, p. 23.

22. Ibid., p. 35; Robert Crandall, *The U.S. Steel Industry in Recurrent Crisis* (Washington: Brookings, 1981), p. 19.

23. *New York Times*, January 6, 1949, p. 1; January 10, p. 13; January 19, p. 30. Also see Henry W. Broude, *Steel Decisions and the National Economy* (New Haven: Yale U. Press, 1963), pp. 16–60.

24. *Republic Steel Corporation Annual Report*, 1947, pp. 4–5.

25. *United States Steel Corporation Annual Report*, 1946, p. 23; 1948, p. 9; 1951.

26. U.S. Congress, House of Representatives, *Hearings before the Subcommittee on Study of Monopoly Power of the Committee on the Judiciary*, 81st Congress, 2nd Session, December 19, 1950 (Washington: Government Printing Office), p. 66.

27. Barnett and Schorsch, *It Could Happen Only in the U.S.* (New York: Time, Inc., 1956), p. 37.

28. Barnett and Schorsch, pp. 23, 27.

29. *Business Week*, November 16, 1963, pp. 144–146.

30. Barnett and Schorsch, pp. 32–33.

31. *Wall Street Journal*, July 29, 1959, p. 1.

32. *Time*, July 20, 1959, p. 94.

33. Adelman, p. 23.

34. McConnell, p. 108.

35. Richard Austin Smith, *Corporations in Crisis* (Garden City, N.Y.: Doubleday, 1963), p. 163.

36. L. L. L. Golden, *Only By Public Consent* (New York: Hawthorn, 1968), p. 17.

37. *New York Times*, April 12, 1962, p. 20.

38. Roger M. Blough, *The Washington Embrace of Business* (New York: Carnegie-Mellon University and Columbia U. Press, 1975), pp. 89, 137–138.

39. Ibid., p. 146; New York Times, April 15, 1962, p. 20.

40. Blough, p. 145.

41. Ibid., p. 148; Kim McQuaid, *Big Business and Presidential Power* (New York: William Morrow, 1982), p. 209.

42. Ibid., p. 149.

43. Golden, p. 4.

44. *Public Relations News*, Aprils 23, 1962.

45. Speech by Roger Blough to Edison Electric Institute in Atlantic City, New Jersey, July 3, 1962.

46. McQuaid, p. 211.

47. Ibid, p. 221.

48. Golden, p. 20.

49. Some statistics on steel imports show the domestic steel industry was becoming uncompetitive during this period: 1957: 1,155,000 net tons imported, 5,348 exported. 1962: 4,100 imported, 2,013 exported. 1967: 11,455 imported, 1,685 exported. (AISI, *Steel Imports—A National Concern* (Washington: 1970), p. 61.

CHAPTER TWELVE
Governmental Relations and
Contributions Policies, 1962–1982

1. See, for instance, interpretation in Golden's *Only by Public Consent*, and Blough's *The Washington Embrace of Business*.

2. Kim McQuaid, *Big Business and Presidential Power* (New York: William Morrow, 1982), p. 231.

3. Lyndon B. Johnson Library, Austin, Texas, White House Central Files (WHCF), Box FGO 810.

4. Lyndon B. Johnson Library, Box EX PL2.

5. McQuaid, pp. 231-2.

6. David Bazelon, *Power in America* (New York: New American Library, 1964), pp. 97-98.

7. Quoted in McQuaid, p. 233.

8. Theodore Levitt, "The Johnson Treatment," *Harvard Business Review*, January-February 1967, p. 121.

9. Lyndon B. Johnson Library, Diary Backup, Box 73.

10. Lyndon B. Johnson Library, WHCF, Box FGO 426.

11. Lyndon B. Johnson Library, WHCF, Box BE 7.

12. Ibid.

13. Quoted in Paul Weaver, "Business Loses the War Against Inflation," draft of book chapter sent by Weaver to author, pp. 5-6.

14. McQuaid, p. 281.

15. Fred Smith, *Wall Street Journal*, January 16, 1986, p. 22.

16. Ibid.

17. For an examination of the spread of corporate philanthropy since that decision, see *Corporate Philanthropy* (Washington: Council on Foundations, 1982).

18. Quoted in David Finn, *The Corporate Oligarch* (New York: Simon and Schuster, 1969), p. 235.

19. Ibid.

20. *Wall Street Journal*, June 28, 1985, p. 20.

21. See Olasky, *The Council on Foundations* (Washington: Capital Research Center, 1985).

22. *Corporate Philanthropy*, p. 3.

23. Quoted in Olasky, "Reagan's Second Thoughts on Corporate Giving," *Fortune*, September 20, 1982, p. 132.

24. Comments made during interviews with the author, Summer 1982.

25. Ibid.

26. Ibid.

27. Ibid.

28. Ibid.

29. Ibid.

30. Ibid.

31. Ibid.

32. *Fortune*, September 20, 1982, p. 136.

33. Quoted in *National Review*, May 15, 1981, p. 545.

34. Interview with the author, 1983.

35. Ibid.

36. *Organization Trends*, November, 1982, pp. 2-4.

37. Charles Wohlstetter, "The Urge to Self-Destruct," speech given at meeting of the International Platform Association, Washington, D.C., August 2, 1984.

CHAPTER THIRTEEN
Ministers or Panderers

1. Ed Lipscomb, "Let's Get Lost," speech delivered November 24, 1952. Published by the Public Relations Society of America. Included in Bateman Papers, Barker Texas History Center, The University of Texas at Austin.

2. Ibid; also Fraser Seitel, *The Practice of Public Relations* (Columbus, Ohio: Charles E. Merrill, 1984), pp. 518–519.

3. Original code contained in Bateman Papers, Barker Texas History Center, The University of Texas at Austin. Current version in Seitel, p. 518.

4. *Public Relations Journal*, January, 1976, p. 13.

5. Scott M. Cutlip, Allen H. Center, Glen M. Broom, *Effective Public Relations*, sixth edition (Englewood Cliffs, N.J.: Prentice-Hall, 1985), p. 461.

6. Bok, p. 260; Cutlip et al., p. 458.

7. See Olasky, "The Amoral World of Public Relations," *Business and Society Review*, Winter, 1985.

8. Ibid.

9. Ibid. These attitudes are probably not new. Twenty-five years ago, in a *Public Relations Journal* article entitled, "Whither the Society's Code," Bruce Watson described some unfavorable signs developing and argued that, "The seeds of future crippling disease would rest in these two conditions: that of indifference to the substance and intent of the Code, and that of failure to act on the part of those who have studied and understand its provisions and who have unmistakable knowledge of its violation. Apathy toward the Code on the one hand, or mute connivance in its perversion, on the other, would quite likely produce opposite results from those for which it was intended. Effective enforcement is the only nourishment by which the Code may be kept alive and healthy." (October, 1960, pp. 23–24)

10. *Public Relations Review*, Fall, 1982, p. 63.

11. See Herbert Schlossberg, *Idols for Destruction* (Thomas Nelson: Nashville, 1983), p. 254.

12. PR, October, 1958, p. 8.

13. Robert Kaus, "There's No Shame Anymore," *Harper's*, August, 1982, p. 10.

14. Ibid., pp. 14, 15.

15. Seitel, p. 518.

16. *Public Relations Journal*, March, 1957, p. 8.

17. Ibid., August, 1958, p. 17.

18. Ibid., June, 1958, p. 23.

19. Ibid.

20. Ibid., February, 1963, p. 7.

21. Ibid., September 1963, p. 6.

22. Ibid., December, 1969, p. 8.

23. Ibid., October, 1971, p. 34.

24. Ibid., October, 1971, pp. 40–41.

25. Ibid., October, 1972, p. 2.

26. Ibid., August, 1974, p. 10.

27. Ibid., February, 1975, p. 24.

28. Ibid., July, 1975, pp. 12–13.

29. See Amos Kendall, *Autobiography* (Boston: Ticknor, 1902), especially p. 175.

30. *Public Relations Journal*, December, 1982, p. 15.

31. *Public Relations Journal*, March, 1981, pp. 24, 27, 34; April, 1981, p. 4. One positive note about the task force's report: It included some common sense comments about the ethical pretension of calling public relations a *profession*: "The question of whether public relations is a profession or on the verge of becoming one is not germane to our considerations. The extensive attention this matter has received reflects the inward orientation of the field that has dominated much of its history. The benefits of esteem as professionals will result from how the publics perceive public relations practitioners, not what they claim to be. In recent years aspiration to be called a 'profession' has become endemic in our society. Countless crafts have, in this age of permissiveness, taken on themselves the claim of being 'professions,' to the point where the term has little meaning except for a few fields that the public has long considered to be professions." (pp. 26–7)

32. Column by Winkelman, *Public Relations Journal*, February, 1985, p. 3.

33. Ibid., p. 8.

34. Ibid, p. 3.

35. Donald McCammond, "The Growth of Ethical Awareness," *Public Relations Journal*, April, 1985, p. 38.

36. Ibid.

37. Ibid, p. 39.

38. Don Hill, "Standing in Loco Clientis," *Public Relations Journal*, June, 1985, pp. 4–5.

39. *Public Relations Journal*, January, 1986, pp. 7–8.

40. Ibid., June, 1973, p. 36.

41. Clipping in Bateman Papers.

CHAPTER FOURTEEN
The Four-Fold Discipline

1. See, for instance, Fraser Seitel, *The Practice of Public Relations*, second edition (Columbus, Ohio: Chas. Merrill, 1984); Craig E. Aronoff and Otis W. Baskin, *Public Relations: The Profession and the Practice* (St. Paul: West Publishing Co., 1983); Scott M. Cutlip, Allen H. Center, Glen M. Broom, *Effective Public Relations*, sixth edition (Englewood Cliffs, N.J.: Prentice-Hall, 1985); Ronald Lovell, *Inside Public Relations* (Boston: Allyn and Bacon, 1982); John E. Marston, *Modern Public Relations* (New York: McGraw-Hill, 1979); Doug Newsom and Alan Scott, *This is PR: The Realities of Public Relations* (Belmont, Ca: Wadsworth, 1981); Robert T. Reilly, *Public Relations in Action* (Englewood Cliffs, N.J.: Prentice-Hall, 1981); Raymond Simon, *Publicity and Public Relations Worktext*, fifth edition, (Columbus, Ohio: Grid Publishing, 1983).

2. Seitel, p. 4. Nor can it be said that the reputation of public relations is low because of a lack of public understanding of the field. A 1981 survey showed 51% of the American adults polled saying they had a "clear idea" or a "general idea" of the kind of work that people in public relations do. Figures for other fields within the "communications industry" were 66% for "people in the press (TV and newspapers)," 59% for "people in advertising," 46% for "people in magazine publishing" and 42% for "people

in book publishing." The field that finished second in professed public understanding, advertising, rated last in esteem; the field that was understood least, book publishing, is generally considered to be highest in esteem of the five fields. (Seitel, p. 91)

3. Lawrence W. Nolte, *Fundamentals of Public Relations* (New York: Pergamon, 1974), p. 9.

4. J. A. R. Pimlott, *Public Relations and American Democracy* (Princeton: Princeton University Press, 1951), p. 202.

5. Pimlott, p. 203. In public relations, blaming the outsiders has become so traditional that even insiders could not resist satirizing the tendency at times. An article in 1974 recommended ways to "blame others. Find a scapegoat. Run an 'us and them' ad – the 'us' being PRSA's pure of heart, the 'them' being the heathens who don't belong." (Dan Forrestal, *PRJ* May, 1974, "Placing Public Relations in Perspective")

6. Many of Leggett's columns have been reprinted in *Democratick Editorials* (Indianapolis: Liberty Press, 1984). Here, p. 11.

7. Ibid.

8. Ibid., pp. 3, 5, 11.

9. Ibid., p. 13.

10. Ibid., p. 3.

11. Ibid.

12. Interview with Company Q's public affairs vice president, 1985.

13. Column on "The Credibility of Corporations" in Bateman Papers.

14. Isadore Barmash, *The World Is Full Of It* (New York: Delacorte Press, 1974), pp. 174-175.

15. Seitel, p. 401.

16. Sissela Bok, *Lying* (New York: Random House, 1978), p. 134.

17. Ibid., p. 149.

18. Ibid., p. 79.

19. Ibid., p. 61.

20. Ibid, pp. 20-21. Although aware of the downward spiral, some continue to think they can be free riders forever. As Bok notes, liars "may believe, with Machiavelli, that 'great things' have been done by those who have 'little regard for good faith.' They may trust that they can make wise use of the power that lies bring. And they may have confidence in their own ability to distinguish the times when good reasons support their decision to lie . . . They may invoke special reasons to lie – such as the need to protect confidentiality or to spare someone's feelings." Yet Bok notes a certain inevitable distortion here: "In this benevolent self-evaluation by the liar of the lies he might tell, certain kinds of disadvantage and harm are almost always overlooked. Liars usually weigh only the immediate harm to others from the lie against the benefits they want to achieve. The flaw in such an outlook is that it ignores or underestimates two additional kinds of harm – the harm that lying does to liars themselves and the harm done to the general level of trust and social cooperation. Both are cumulative; both are hard to reverse." (pp. 23-24)

21. Henry Adams, *The Education of Henry Adams* (Boston: Houghton-Mifflin, 1961), p. 9. Richard Weaver once noted that unless professors are "resigned to the teaching of sophistry or of etiquette, there remains only the severe and lofty discipline of *vere loqui*. This means teaching people to speak the truth, which can be done only by

giving them the right names of things . . . every teacher is for his students an Adam. They come to him trusting in his power to bestow the right name on things." (*Language is Sermonic*, Louisiana State University Press: Baton Rouge, La., 1970, pp. 191-192)

22. Alan Harrington, *Life in the Crystal Palace* (New York: Knopf, 1959), p. 183.

23. Ibid., p. 180.

24. Ibid., pp. 180, 183-4.

25. Personal interview, July, 1983.

26. Ibid.

27. Ibid.

CONCLUSION
A Word to Corporate Executives

1. Seitel, p. 401.

2. *Public Relations Journal*, November, 1972, p. 66.

INDEX